On the Edge of the Field
Poems

Evolving Through Eight Years on the Art Farm

by

Richard Sievers

On the Edge of the Field

Copyright © 2018 Richard Sievers

All Rights Reserved

Field of Seven Houses Publishing
fieldofsevenhouses.blogspot.com
sailingspiritwinds.blogspot.com
ricksfarm@yahoo.com

ISBN:

Print Edition: **978-0-9829207-5-6**

Electronic Edition: 978-0-9829207-6-3

Library of Congress Control Number: **2017907134**

For

My Beloved Friends

The diversity of your love and kindness has caused me to remain and to be free.

On the Edge of the Field
Table of Contents

Fourth Year

Fifth Year

Sixth Year

Seventh Year

Eighth Year

After the Move

Prologue

These poems are the recordings of my journey from neophyte farmer and father to a more seasoned and solid soul. These words are the chronicle of eight years working on and stewarding an organic farm in the Pacific Northwest of the USA. I wrote most of these poems in an old cabin, sitting behind a picture window above the farm and pasture. You may notice how the first entries reflect a steep learning curve on how to be a sensitive man in an intense world of parenting, marriage and business. For these were my first years inhabiting all three of these labels. These years began with hope and idealism. They end with both losing the farm and gaining a much deeper set of inner resources to be alive and to be of service.

Thank you for reading these excerpts from my inner and outer journey as a farmer. The words and sentiments, however, are not ultimately intended to be just about my particular journey. They are intended as reflections on how we all navigate the birth, life and endings of any dream. May these poems bring healing for you in whatever endeavor that you commit to, no matter how wild and off the grid they may be.

I learned much from the farm. For instance, all things on earth move in a seasonal circle of spring, summer, autumn and winter. This book is really about the autumnal harvests in the maturing life. It's about the tilling, planting, caring and harvesting of any intention or endeavor. May your seasons and your callings and your goodbyes be blessed by these words.

Rick

Note on wording.

Reclaiming and using the word *God* in a spirit of inclusivity:

Throughout this book I have endeavored to contact what is sacred. Along with words like *Beloved, Mystery, Presence, Spirit* etc. I have also used the word *God*. I have used it as a seasoning and soothing throughout the text. For those who have experienced a sadness or trauma in connection with this word please forgive me. And please feel free to replace it with whatever metaphor, idea or name that brings a welling of joy, hope and love. I have used this word purposefully. I also included this because I could not intuit another adequate personal substitute.

I also have intended to use the word as an act of inclusivity and healing. Unlike many religious doctrines I have few illusions of absolute truth, or gender, or anthropomorphism regarding God. I use the name as a way to reclaim what has been taken away from us for many generations. I use it as a way to reclaim the mystery of the universe and as a way to counter-act dogma.

The certain, the powerful and the self-righteous have no exclusive right to any sacred name. Foolishly I put my sights on trying to decipher the Great Mystery, trying to describe what is truly indescribable. I think that every poet/artist/lover is just trying to describe the great sun of love with the little shattered mirrors of words.

Thank You.

First Year

Window, Gate, Field
June 6

This window facing south.
My spirit hovering in the north.
Outside of my reach,
lies the remnant field
of a once forgotten farm.

An angel took me
to heaven in the dark
season of my boyhood,
then brought me back
to earth,
as a man,
on this farm,
facing this meadow.

Look into my eyes.
See the rows
of apple and plum
planted around a bowl of night
and a glistening horde of stars.
Feel the grasses
along the shimmery fence line
bent with diamonds of rain.
Hear the metal gate
swinging its rusty sing song.
Enter my home.
Enter my treasure.

Our First Night in Our New-Old Home

Pearl
June 9

We slept in the piles of the living room.
The farm house, a silent cave.
The dogs howled outside.
A visitor arrived on the early morning,
turning her gnarled fingers in the dew.

An old woman stood above us.
Watched us awaken.
She was grey as the winter,
long hair, nightgown, sleepy eyed,
shocked to see us here.
She held her palsied hand to her lips.
Her eyes were both
surprised and accepting.
"Oh my, I must be dead."
she said to herself.
Then she faded into the night.

Yes, my dear, you are dead.
I sit by your prized window
watching your silver barn turn
to rust in the June gloom.
The descendants of your robins
still hunt with the quizzical cock
of their heads. Your peonies
unfold and shimmer like your gown
when you were young and in love.

Your field still rolls
in green waves of the wind.
And your chipped sink still draws
out dreams with the splash
and clank of dishes.

I'm guessing you noticed the wall
I tore out between
your kitchen and the rest
of your house.
Your kitchen was
so much like a cage.
Now it's splayed wide open.
Now the wind moans, the cat plays,
and children run through
your house with ease.

You, wrinkled old matron,
are free to go to your own Elysian Fields.
Thank you.
Fly through the openings we have made.
The moon is waxing.
Go to the light.
Tear through the darkness.

We'll trim your roses,
scythe your field.
Soon enough we will follow
you home.

Holy Things
For Heather
June 12

Holy things show
themselves through surprise,
being both transient and unalterable.

Like the island rising
over the shoulder of road
when I was lost.

Your glowing face
at the airport curb.

This white farmhouse
I'd passed by
for years.

A poem at the edge
of waking, before
the newspaper hit the driveway.

The perfume of the river
as we flew our open
windows across the bridge.

Sunlight spearing
a crystal through
our breakfast table.

A covey of quail
in the snowberry.

The foghorn
I heard two hundred
miles from the sea.

The home I dreamed
of moments before
I woke in your arms.

We Are The Earth

June 23

The field's dandelions know.
So do the martins, green as the belt of forest.
The coyotes in the trickling shadow of the creek bed understand.
So it is with the mouse carefully scanning for the talon of a red tail in a cerulean sky.
We are the earth, and never separate.

What we walk upon, we become.
Remember the verdant earth we are made of,
the earth we rose from,
the earth to which we will return.

A million years from now this field will still be here and so will I.
My flesh clad in baked soil.
Memories will spin in the writhing joy of the fox
hopping into a vision above the river of grasses.
Perhaps an ocean will cover this ground.
Or a glacier will grind me into powder.

All the bones and fur,
the echoes of love making,
the alarmed chirps of the cotton tail
will be here
and so will I.

This wild practice of heaven
is just a wide eyed walk in the field,
and we will live here forever.

Forms come and go…
this grass,
this day,
this sun,
this holding of hands in the burning light,
this tired rolling mind.

All of it will sink,
slow and sure beneath the ocean of flowers.
That is the assurance of our sacred world.
That is our heaven and hell.
That is our birthright and deathbed.

We are this field darting with dragon flies.
We are of the earth,
no matter what the mind fools us into believing.

Our Summer Ghost is Waning
August 28

Friend, you drift away
with the season.
Then you return,
like you left, in autumnal surprise.
Perhaps I dreamt you
back from the dead.
There you were,
sitting in the alcove of my cabin,
my precocious childhood friend.
Rest awhile on this inland island.
We can talk about what our life
would be like now
that you are alive again.

You and me and my family together.
Strange comfort even to my lover,
now that you breathe again,
smiling in the coffee breeze sun,
gleaming in the hand prints
smudged on the cabin window.
Why do you haunt us?
Please stay.

My beloved flits about
the house across the field,
a shining stranger
to this world. She has
her sister back home,
her shadow, her doppelganger.
Now we're all in this passion
play together.

All I know is that I feel
part of my soul has returned home.
The sun in the streaked window,
the chatter of the forest,
scratch of the pen on paper are all
whispering the name
once left silent in the earth.

What Matters Now
September 8

What matters now
is the eagle
hidden by the ink
of the night sky,
the coyote
stretching from her den
after a day of sleeping,
the snake
warming herself beneath
a stone on the edge of the arroyo.

What matters now
is that I am breathing
all of these beings alive,
thinking not in words,
though my hand writes
and knows the heart of the words.

No mind is vast
enough for God's voices.
Yet we can be the eagle
or the coyote or the snake.

Move out into
your animal life,
with no plan tonight
except to dance through
the silvered slivers
of moonlight.

There is no river to ford.
The sand is still
warm and moist
from yesterday's stormy sun.
There's no second thought
of last night's dream of mice
running in fields of mesquite.
All the animals with the urge
to follow their senses,
scribe a path
mostly unseen by others.

I am free in this world
as you are free,
my friend.
Let us awaken from
the faults of seriousness
and dive straight into the dark.

There are a million strands of
precious silver leading you
into a new adventure,
leading you into the canyons
and the brooding stillness of mountains,
into the quaking cottonwood forest song.

Awe lives here.
And you will find
that you live here too,
home in the night and free.

Today After the Storm
September 27

Today I will
gaze upon the field.
Today I will
do the work of watching.
Today I will
be still and remember reverently
the wild night
we just passed through.

I will
be free to watch.
I will
be more than happy
and less than sad.

See the single scarlet
leaf, maple's last flutter
of autumn's song.

Hear the crystal
bowl of earth
ripple within the sun streams.

Touch the frosted
footfalls, weaving
tales of last night
into the grass.

Daylight has come.

The curling fist
of the storm
is now an open hand.
Pull the blinds upward.
Invite your eyes
into the wide and the blue.

The problems can wait.
The chores and sweat can wait.
The doings will rest.
The field is enough.

The Rain

October 15

The rain is chattering
upon my dusty roof,
falling upon the light
of my mind,
streaming with the sun
of my song,
writing in the mud
of my fallow garden,
filling the cracks once
dry with summer's wanting skies.

Rushing Through

October 22

Look at the long shadows
and the sun reddened leaf
falling upon the field.
Frost on the blueberry.
Wild cherry sparkling miniature suns.
Consider the moments of silence
between the moaning cars and the barking dogs.
Sky, blue as your eyes,
wide as your net of praise.
The wind being a song
rushing through your fingers.

19

Mist
November 2

Mist is my companion.
Fog of sleep,
now rising.
Mist, my lost longing,
my lover leaving
on her way to
kiss the face of the sun.
Mist, my heart
of the sea,
now hung over
the long verdant body
of the field.

Mist, the grey
blue star of morning.
Now the sun.
Now the cloud.
Now the river.
Now winter's song.
Life is one,
hidden and then
revealed in
a wheel
of days and nights.

Mystery
November 3

Now the field is
an ocean of light.
Now the sun spirals are
eddies and
whirlpools.
Now frozen time
is thawed.

I am islands
and desert spires.
I am the sleeper awakened.
I am the spirits of
mountain stone
outside my window.
I am the window.
I am the grasses.

The shadow dancers are
tumbling in from the coast.
Our eyes are a field of
brooding grey and
sunflower yellow of autumn.

Dawn has passed us by.
The night is a dream.
The afternoon is only a place
to be born.
Here we are between
all of that.

There is no "there" out there.
~
And if you can wrap
your head around
what I'm saying
then you may be crazy too.
Perhaps *Mystery* is
a sense all to itself.

The Cabin Song
November 17

It's not the fog
or how the sun stirs his holy hands
through the morning.
It's not the gold and pewter
of the field, framed
with the symphony of knotty pine.
It's not the coffee waft
of crystal rainbows.
It's not the rusted mantle and
wrinkled brick of the chimney
standing sentinel.

Outside, the silver jewel box barn
shimmers with a memory
of the ancient forest.
The army of trees marches
right to the edge
of the coyote's wink of sleep.

My eyes reflect
the steamy windows.
The meaning of everything
is clear without words.
Yet I try telling it
with words anyway.

The winter has fallen
upon the highlands.
I wait here on the edge
of the white haired field.

Out there, somewhere,
my family is:
at school,
on the river,
traveling the highway through
the Great Rift,
asleep in front of a flickering screen.

I am here at the window.

There are so many ways
to embrace and release time.
There are so many ways
to sing succulence
into this life.

I want you to know,
that we are fine, simply
being here in this world.
I am watching all of you,
my beloveds.

We are free!

See the spiral of wind in the grasses?
See the wheel of Orion's eyes at midnight?
I'll be hovering somewhere
in-between both,
with you, and waiting
for you to come home.
Time is our palette of infinite color.

Live free dear friends,
upon the Earth:
wives,
mothers,
singing land,
island home,
memory of self.

This is only the beginning.
See the light upon
the field?
Go.
Dance there.
Be wonder-full
as much as you can.

There is no other life
that can be your own.

Six Months on the Farm
November 30

And it's growing on me.

Loosen one shirt.
Wear another.

The man, real in this life,
until his skin is loosened too.

The Forever Autumn
Such a Beauty Day
December 4

Such a beauty day.
Chainsaw singing in the forest.
Chimney smoke scrying upon the sky.
Starlings feeding in waves in the field.
Stream swirling diamonds in a bowl of alder root.

Nothing is permanent?
I'm not so sure of this so tritely stated *truth*.

This thin line stretches on forever,
this sun warming my hand,
this wind winding through my hair,
can come with me
if I invite them with love.
Only love,
no clinging allowed.

Softened

December 24

There are secrets you can only learn
from a softened heart,
like how to say
"beloved, beloved, beloved"
as you sit with her pain,
and your own.

It's 2 AM and the hearth needs fuel.
The house is cold.
The children are sick.
But you get up,
load up the woodstove,
talk with the stirred up teenager,
hold your aching partner.

Then everyone goes back
to their dreaming.

All you thought
you wanted was to sleep.
Then the quiet wakefulness descends
as the hearth groans back to life.

You step outside.
A star, as blue
as the solstice night, blinks
in the iris of the rushing clouds.
The chimney casts a net of smoke
drifting into an icy sea.

All the thought lights are turned off now.

Everyone is safe
in bed but you.
Everywhere is safe
now for you.
You light a candle
in the frozen lantern on the lintel
of your cabin door.
You see the little flame,
remembering the star
and the soft face
you just kissed.

You know everything
that is important
now.
All the faces of the one
true God, and the eye of love
winking above, the soft
flicker of awe lighting
the entry way below.

Everything is holy now.
The faces of God
rest in your home.
The smoke
of the hearth is singing
in the ice colored night.
And you are no longer
longing for sleep.

Second Year

Garden Prayer
April 19

Walk with me beloved.
Make this garden like the first.
Let me hold your hand and kiss your face.
Let the animals lie down beside us as we ponder rain drops.
Let us share the sweet good fruits of these happily laden apple trees.
Let us laugh until we cry with some joyous joke that only we understand.
Be with me in the garden, beloved.
Let us be lovers unashamed.
Let me wipe your tears away.
Let me name the deer that you have formed from the same clay, stone and sunlight as me.
Let us worship sacred love as we look into each other's eyes.
Walk with me in the garden… this innocence like the first.

The Trick to Farming Poems and Other Crops
May 14

The trick is
to not view the field
as a piece of work
for development.

The trick is
to be with the land,
to husband it and
to be its wife.

The trick is
to be still
in the planning and
the hoeing.

The trick is
to celebrate what is
alive at the moment
while visioning
the possibilities.

The trick is
to sow love
before the seed goes
in the ground.

The trick is
to tend the body
of the earth through
the long summer and
to reap gratitude
with whatever
harvest comes.

Farm Light
May 16

It's hard not to work in the summer morning sunlight.
A cool stream is waiting there, just past the field,
on the edge between shade and fever.

Bee Song
For Jacqueline
May 30

A bee swings by,
sashaying
through the pale
grove of strawberry flowers.
She sings.
I hear her,
like a faint tune
on the radio next door,
on the other side
of the beaten hedge
of cedar.

I hear a song
I cannot quite make out.
I listen deeper.
I wonder when I'll know
the words,
when I can
sing what the bee knows
by heart.

Planting a Poem
June 22

The way to harvest
means balance
between planting
thick enough to push
out the weeds and
sowing an excess
for the ones that will fall
due to moles, bugs and
other inattentions.

Then leaving room
for growth,
nurturing what is
fruitful and healthy.
Dispatching what limps
and shrivels.
Finally taking out all
persistent interlopers,
the invaders of
mandible, thorn and tendril.

A garden contains
the growing and
the space to grow.

Smoke
July 1

The dearly departed
ghosts of a California
forest float in our sky.
The homes and dreams
of ten million creatures
hang in our nostrils.

Blood orange winds blaze,
a sky root of the Great
Mother Tree withers.

Between the lovers and
users of earth
are the animals and plants.

Here we are
in the middle
with them.

Pray to God
for courage.
Pray to His Wife,
The Earth, for mercy.

At the Dance in the City Without You
July 10

The dancing was a writhing sweat.
So many women
watching and searching.
One looks like you,
though younger.
Her desert eyes,
deep and lonely,
meeting my oceanic glances.

I turn away from her,
remembering that you're home
with the children while I dance
free, a man all in black
pretending to be
of the city.

The country claims me
now with her coveralls and sawdust,
sickles in alfalfa,
roosters at dawn,
and a scarred cat scratching
at the barn door.

My once city eyes turn north,
remembering how
we drink in the starry nights
as we sip beer on the back porch.

You and I are
the dancers in the dark mantle
that hovers above our orchard,
we the committed,
we the field
and the freeway home.

Through the Heat
July 17

It's a day steeped in flames
where the rusty dog's spirit is too dry to bark,
where the tap tap tap of the sprinkler
offers its reward in a song from childhood.
It's the hot of shuttered houses,
the hot of bright clothes bleached
pale and limp on the clothesline.

The scorching smoke from the dying forest
pushes a drowsy drug into the paralyzed dream of the afternoon.
The boiling moon rises in ripples unquenched.
All the creatures panting in faint breaths
come down the canyons in search of our withering pond.

Draped beside the apple tree,
my lover, with eyes closed,
observes a cooler country
on the other side
of the sun.

Then she opens and gazes up
through the branches heavy with fruit.
Her hand anchored to the back of my neck.
Sweat conducting lightning between our skin.
The smoke rises as she strokes up the moon,
her burning fingers trembling in my hair.

Heat, light and longing,
these are true,
these are real.

Only One Thing
September 9

I am sitting at the desk.
Stalking the movement of light on the forest edge with my eyes.
The blue heaven framed in misted windows.
Fingers of fog stretching from the field.
Creek chattering with her rolling stones.
The alder already shining with their golden faces, reflecting summer's dying fire.

I'm here, waiting for words, waiting for something to happen.
Ink staining my hands, calling for something novel and inspiring.
The cat sitting on the desk too, watching for prey in the garden below.

Me, inhabiting the same primal meditation.

Waiting all my life for something to happen.
Waiting for some spirit I can capture, consume and resurrect.
When all along
the green and yellow flames of the forest,
the budding and scarlet heavens,
the white and purple sea have sent me gifts,
saying:

> *Open this offering, thinker.*
> *Open this window, traveler.*
> *Open your eyes, singer.*
> *Open your heart, lover.*
> *Only one thing is ever happening.*
> *Do you know what it is?*

Drifting in Anacortes
February 26

Alone at a table for four.
Green copper and
frayed sails drape the walls.
An old sailor's shanty song
steams from the kitchen.

I have nowhere to go
but back to the farm today.
I came here to find
my island inspiration and
found that it was
already in my shirt pocket.
I thought I'd lost
the fire in my heart.
I thought I'd burned down
the cinnamon scented forest.

The sails are hung
limp upon the walls of this café.
They yearn for the wind outside.
They dream of another world.

Through my sun whipped
window a breeze lifts my page.
The paper flutters,
fills with spirit wind,
fills with storms and
floats with seagulls above
tides and amber waves.

Sails are for flying.
Pages are for filling.
Islands are for worshiping
all that is free and beautiful.
This page flutters in the wind.
This breath is a flood and ebb.
This heart swells.
This hand is weathered from all the knots
they have tied and then loosened.

I make my own words now,
pouring them into the sea and
the field of stars. I am just a man
alone in a sleepy fisherman's café.
The windows rattling my mind
with a promise.

Old sailor's yarns are unraveling,
along with my self-control,
adrift in the tides,
pulled by the weight of beauty,
moored to the rocky swelling of the sea
sweetened with salt.

I am alone as an island
appears to be alone.
I am a specter and
a sailor of the heart,
adrift in Poseidon's dreams,
flying fast before the yard arms singing.

The island of my youth was
a lure to get me somewhere
clear, so I could see my own life.
Like the grail or Avalon,
a quest inducing vision that landed
me in my body, a vessel
which is strong and
fragile on the tides.

God of fire rise in the sun.
God of earth be my mountain.
God of water hold me in a place
between doom and glory.
God of wind song
bring me home
to myself.

Floating Out the Window
March 2

A jet plane is wheeling
through the high
cloud bank like a leaf
bouncing down
a great grey river.
The engine pulses
its way northward.

The pilot already sees
the ocean I can only feel.

At my window,
set in its crooked
frame, here
above the field
where the robins play,
here is my earth.

I am spinning
in spirals and floating
through the pane.

I am in wonder
about the pilots
at the plane's controls,
imagining them
as they gaze out the portholes
from their fragile craft.

Their windows cover
such wide trajectories of sight,
yet they hold no more
beauty than this cabin's fragile glass.

Flying high or falling
in love with the ordinary,
it's all the same.

How good it is to live!
How good it is to witness
what is right here,
close to the dewy grass,
bent with the lucky
burden of growth.

I Write I Prune I Light
March 17

I prune the great
pear tree burdened
with twisted scions,
slicing suckers
shadowing the fruiting
branches.

Wooden fragments lie
all around the trunk now.
But the surviving branches are
now lit with morning fire.

The shadow is healed.
The moldering is soothed.
The oozing braches are poised
for new growth.

Only a Moment in This World
April 10

A spider web is floating on the wind,
one end still tethered to the eave of the house,
the other end flying all the way across the garden.
A delicate spider rides the filament
even as the cord snaps in mid-air.
She rides the remnant of that string
into the other world.

I watch the silver silk,
so strong for moments,
as it flies and curves in upon itself,
shattering the sun into a thrumming
pulse of wind.

A blue jay sings for his supper.
He spies the thread and its passenger.
Then he swoops down with wings like an angel.
He eats the sun silvered pilot of silk.

I just watch,
floating in my thoughts,
weaving a story attached, for now,
to my head.
A breeze lifts my soul
out and beyond the world,
back to the garden
where angels sing and hover.

Only a moment in the wind and then…

Spring Garden Spring Sadness
April 28

A sun-blade cuts diamonds
across the green
face of the meadow.
Then it is gone.
A smile rises
behind the tear.
All day I'd rushed
into the rain
to tend the straining
crop of beauty.

Field of sky, finally
I hear your roots reaching and
your buds swelling,
even as the neighbor's tractor is humming
destruction around your edges.

Outside, the chickens peck
blithely, not knowing
that their death is only spared
by my intervention
of stones thrown at predatory eyes and
fences bent straight again.

For now, the field is safe.
For now, the world is soft.
For now, it is only morning.

The sky stretches out
through the window,
beyond rolling cloud banks.
The sun is really not so far away now.

My love, I have waited for you
at this window.
I see you.
I am here.

Passing Grace
May 18

The rain tumbles
in grey and white locks
of God's great benevolence,
pissing grace all
over the muddy garden.
The field becoming a fertile, soggy soup
for the rotting root and
the singing frog.

The Sacrifice Area

June 15

The round garden
floats upon the old
corral, the sacrifice area,
where animals once muddied
and denuded the earth.
Their constant pacing,
defecation and boredom
infused the muck,
making a compacted sterility.
So I placed the garden
in this saddest aspect
of the once fertile field.

The field has been a meadow
again for years.
But the garden space languished
with soil hard as adobe.
Now the corners are light
with crimson clover,
rebuilding the hidden
communities of light and loam.

This is my home,
once scorched and
infused with abuse.
This place feeds me
from the windows above.
In this place I make
my stand, asking
for patience in
the healing and growth.

In Time
June 22

In time…
        Now is the time.
Someday…
        Today is the day.
Over there…
        Somewhere is here.

This is not the life I dreamt…
        It is the life that dreams me awake.

Garden weedy, house broken, phone silent, man needy and wanting.
These are all me too.
Where to begin?
        Now,
        Here,
        Me.

After Awhile
June 24

After a while you don't see
the dimmed shine of the window frame
you once set with care.
The glimmering varnish of the table
is suddenly seven years old and
full of impressions from a pen
that spent itself
in burnt up books.

And you realize you've lived
free of a cubicle job for fifteen
turns around the solar system.
Suddenly you're fifty,
not like thirty
when you smirked
and drank and screwed.

Now, you contemplate the garden.
You pray for the dog that is
barking in your dreams.
You look around your tattered old cabin
and see your old self.
All the sweat of laying
up the knotty pine,
all the to-do lists,
all the scribbling on plywood,
that's all the jetsam of life.
Your memory is the sea.
Your attention is a shattered
sky of broken clouds.

Suddenly your mother is aged.
Your own mornings are achy.
The dreams of a wildwood island
are dusted off and set
into the idea of home again.
How long have you
yearned to live past
the meanness of this world?
And how has the love of your gaze
changed this one, precious,
fleeting life?

After My First Book Was Published

For Callie
August 2

Mostly I sit
with the cat
purring.
Looking outside,
I see our reflections
in the glass.

The trees are flocked
with mist.
The garden is
bent with dew.
The sun is up there,
polishing the granite
of sky, turning it
into pure lapis
and shimmering gold.

I am a cloudy day
full of words and colors.
Soon I will be
a poem.
Soon I will shine.

Another Perfect Day
August 3

My Island I'm coming home.
My island I do not own.
My island is roaming the tides,
while I am anchored still
in the silence of the dark earth.

Time after light, how many summer days left like this?

Another morning above the field with the books and the music flowing all around in the coffee steam. Another day with the page empty and then filled! Ghosts come and then are burned off by the sun. Another sun scorched man runs through the memories.

I'm already itching to get to work doing something useless. While outside the window the good neighbors and their tractors begin their routes in spirals. Am I like them? Dogs begin their howls as sirens pass. I'm passing too. Somewhere in my skull is a grave full of thoughts, clay and worms and roots. Is this beautiful transience what I wanted?

Yes!

Yet all I have I do not own.

Another summer day on earth. Another morning of splashing ink upon the page, watching it fly. This very page will burn like the sun if you let it. Meanwhile the plans for *busyness* pile up in the clippings outside.

I once longed to fly to somewhere like here, to a someday like today.

Raisin Bran
August 17

I don't want
to start the day
just thinking.

A spiraling bowl
of dreams,
a round garden,
a golden globe
of sunflower,
lie before me
shinning.

Starlight is Still There in the Daytime

Even If You Do Not See It
August 28

Garden in sun salutation,
bending up into the eyes of summer,
a lover for the harvest god.
Wind tapping the willow across the window,
brushing the eyes of a believer, fainting into new visions.

I tell the family that I will sit at this desk for hours today.
I'm really flying out above the field,
praising the wings of August,
feeling the persistent tug of a song from the prairie,
being pulled outward, inward, winging my way
into the oblivion of happiness,
then coming home to the corn and pumpkin and potatoes,
coming back to the garden of laughing green
eyes and sparkling hair of gold.

The dead rise up from the roots that embrace their bodies,
shimmering in the leaves that flutter in the wind,
singing their daydreams to rabbits, robins and me,
caressing the starlight from behind the rapture of blue bright sky sun.
I've lived my entire life to land
upon this moment, this day, this season.
In another fifty years I'll still be here as I fling
my starlit eyes all around the sun spun sky.

Together All Alone

September 21

Looking out
across the field
I see the sky lifting
her filigree of fog above the trees.
The morning is a shy woman
hitching up her skirt
before she sits down.
Then she delicately holds
her tea of cinnamon warmth.
Her eyes close softly
above the steam.
The perfume
of leaves wafting and
curling around her face.
We rest in silence,
together all alone.

Sun Mist Storm Clarity
October 28 – November 2

October 28:   What is done lives forever.
All the hidden acts
of respect or hate
or love or war will be seen.
Today I choose love.

October 30:   I am alone and yet surrounded
by all of you who read this.
If I breathe or die
it is all for the service
of that single spark between us,
inflaming the heavens and the sun spun
seed that dreams in the dark
spaces within days.

October 29:   I write because
I write because I write
because I write I write.

October 31:   I lay down the ink again.
The storm from a southern
ocean releases her sunlit
tantrum in dark thunder.
Alone, I write for no
one and every one.
The great book is
one book. Many writers are
jewels in the hand of one singer.
We shine even in the shadowed
light of approaching fists of clouds.

November 1:   A single lamp burns
in my window
above the field.
You may not see
it now, but a single
light is all there is.

November 2:   Filled with poems
instead of thoughts.
Drawn into the field
to the golden maple,
a sun rising in the fog.
Above the flaming crown
a clear blue mind of heaven.

Bear in the Fire of Rain

November 15

Rain all night,
heavy upon the forest canopy.
Congealed drops thunder
ponderously off the needles,
a tapotement of fingers
and claws scratching
runes upon the roof.

Liquid fire is burning
in my dreams, where
a bear is stumbling
with a torn paw distended
with pain. The fierce sow
turns to me in the gloom
of the fog and speaks to me:

"This life is all you have.
This one life.
This one life."

She turns on rippling
haunches and lumbers
into the valley brambles.

She leaves me in our bed,
asleep, floating beside the open
window, soothed with the hissing
steam of the ancient radiator.

In the gloaming light my beloved
spouse is turning her hands
in space as she sleeps.
She is tumbling through a thicket,
a faint arc of a burning scar
is slashed through
the palm of her hand,
shaped into a blazing
rune of secrets
that only the forest can recall.

Bone Fragment
November 17

It happens along the way.
A small chip of bone
gets lodged in the deep
song of the throat.
A gasping life takes in
air that eddies around the fragment.
There is a dream, a memory
that can't quite be
swallowed or brought
out into the fading
night air.

Storms whistle past
the dead, unnoticed
by the femurs and mandibles
wedged beneath our winter garden.
The ghosts add their weight
to the golden roots reaching
deep into the black
pool hovering cold and
sightless, down there,
deep, down
in the earth.

The words are shuttered inside the darkness
and have nowhere to go.
No one hears the heart
of the earth anymore.
        No one will notice
                the cracking crust
                of this glorious world
                        until the mountains quake
                        and the bejeweled cities fall.

Winter Work
December 6

Watching at the window again.
A whole day in front of me.

A crimson blue
kestrel alights on a shattered
branch above the rumpled
sheets of grass and mud that is our field.
She observes and spies.
Finding no prey, she flies on,
searching and waiting, again,
doing the only work
she knows.

Walking From the Henhouse with Eggs in My Pocket
December 7

Carrying eggs in my pocket
up from the long field of frost.
Six little worlds huddled in my coat.
Sun in the grass once
became crying chickens,
laying down their potential and
giving their life back for us.

And we offer our summer
grain back to them,
scooped from the bin
with loving attention.
A fair exchange of worlds,
worlds without end.
Is heaven any different?

Fourth Year

Dream – Awake 1:26 AM
Iduna
January 2

These words are only shadows of an otherworld poem.

Dream Imaginal Setting: A bright and happy day. Meadow lark singing. Raven burbling. The Beloved One moving like a lit singing cloud in the waist high grasses. She wears a simple peasant dress the color of bloodstone. Her hair the color of flax, ochre, and velvet butter. She walks beside the old apple tree along the line of a stone wall. She sings:

I began as an idea.
Then fancied myself
a song fruit
hanging on the sun branch.
More and less than before.
I fell off the tree of stars.
I rest in the field,
past the border of knowing.

Take me into the desire of your mouth.
Oh Beloved, choose me!
I am now only the story
of the world,
tending as all stories do
toward silence.

Last Night the Neighbor Left Footprints
January 3

Last night the neighbor
left footprints pressed
in the crystalline frost.
A perfect V meandered
to and from the center
of our field.

The telltale signs showed a shuffle
in front of our garden gate,
then returning in a beeline
of some cold errand.
The tracks of midnight's
mysterious purpose
remained clear as day
in the frost heaves
of sunrise.

What stories can be deciphered
from the disappearing night?
Who watches in our dreams?
Footprints leave unknowable stories
of what could have been.
Tracks are all that remain
of the midwinter travelers.

It's morning.
The visitor has gone.
Their traces remain.

Asking the Same Old Thing

January 6

Forest backlit by fog.
Dark embers of shadow
burning the branches.
Swoosh of the storm
burying bramble and root.
Animals asleep and shivering
in their dens:

       coyote,
       rabbit,
       vole,
       owl.

Why am I
sad here in a
warm chair
beside memories and trifles?

The sky lies heavy
upon the roof.
The cloud song is
a frozen chant,
preserving all that
ever was and yet
never meant to last.

Ah, spirits,
why did I lose my way?
Where are the days
bright with promises?
Where is the sound
of your claw
upon the roof?
Where are you
now?

Rain Dream Trilogy
January 15 – 17

1.

Sky Wider Than Dreams
January 15

The sky is
a steady circle of flooding
wind beating on the window.
The blue light is glowing
above the pile of books
beside the bed.
Everybody is asleep,
but me. My pen is
moving the twilight
from one end of this
little life of ours
to the next.

The moan of the rigging,
the halyard's song
from the island port
are lifetimes away,
and receding fast.
Ice motes in the tail
of a comet streak by
in burdened drops
of flood and ebb.
The window weeps.
The light flickers.
The night becomes deep,
and wider than any
dreams that stalk me.

2.

Pineapple Express
A warming winter storm brought up from the tropics
January 16

Steady rain.
A sweet breeze
from the islands
of the sun.

A distant bell rings in
the tinkle of chimes.
Drifts of salt and sand
fall off of my dreams.
Rustling fields of cane,
circling sigh of palm,
sticky honey of jasmine,
all move up above
our muddy trails,
then down through
our sagging gutters.

The sky breathes in and
then exhales the memory
of Pele's shore.
A sacred breath was
lifted from a world away,
up into the trade winds,
down through a wilted field,
into my window,
reminding every wondering
islander inside of me
that we're not alone.

3.

They Come In Waves
January 17

They come in waves.
Clouds dream of the land they rose from.
They fall in streams.
Sky dances bright.
The clean eyes of all the ancestors,
my brothers and sisters, are
a mist upon my shoulders,
a soothing kiss upon my brow.

Birth Announcement
January 31

Every day I sit within the frame of this window above the field, beside the bed strewn with poetry, within the comfort of books and a snoring cat. Life is real today because of the miracle of sitting still and seeing. This is the work of the lost. This is the work of a simpleton. I am just another singer of little everythings. I wear a necklace of stars. I am the dancer of bent grasses, God's child of flooded fields and sun streams, beloved of heaven and of earth.

Do You Hear the Rainbow?
March 8

Do you hear the rainbow singing in the quivering cloud, in the rustle of the curtained breeze? Can you decipher the warm moan of earth rising into spring? Did you travel all this way to be a seed in the dark? Pilgrim, be at home! Be the pleasure of the field. The grasses know you. The mountain remembers you. The desert prays for you. The Mystery is already leading you back to the still point. Wherever you are, remember you are known, in the center of it all. You are heaven longing for itself. Take from this place what you could not take in childhood. Be in the silence. Give to this place what is not received by the sleeping: the dreamer's song, the joy of silence, being anything you want to be. This world is a gift for you, and you are a gift for the world. We breathe in a perfect circle within infinite directions. Claim your home on earth, as it is in heaven.

But the Weather Report Said
Dry and Clearing
March 21

Water etches the window,
fills the field with tears,
floods the downspout with a tinkling song,
inundates my eyes with sleepy wondering.

Who am I
if not a spiraling flare
of a hidden star,
a particle of a shimmering God,
a sunlit eye of the rain?

Brightness Flying in the Wind
March 29

I cannot live
like I've lived before.
Withering
if I do not write,
if I do not pray.

I am hounded by the muse,
pushed down onto the bed
as she screams:
Let me out. Let me out.

The robin outside my window
is singing my childhood
back home to me.
I want to feel like
I once felt.

But there's an ache
of reservation,
an icy sickle of resignation
tapping on the shoulders
of my dreams.

I am the end
of the world.
I've resisted what is true.
I am a stately house
built on rotting pilings
in sinking sand.

I am called outside
of my skyward foundation,
spiraling down a social sink
of angry people, disconnections,
divisions and discontent,
falling into the worries
of the suffering
and the shopping malls
of bewildered consumption.

I cannot navigate between
this dead merchandise and
the need to practice
the cadence of my beating heart.

People want something
from me that I cannot
give: surety, comfort.

What can I do
to counter weight
the scales of insecurity?

> *Lift*
> *your arms out and fly.*
> *Be*
> *the robin*
> *exposed in the field.*
> *Sing*
> *your spring love song.*
>
> *This is all you need to do:*
> *Spread your wings*
> *and allow the wind*
> *to carry you.*
>
> *You are good enough,*
> *high enough and*
> *free enough to*
> *reflect the sun,*
> *become the moon,*
> *and love the earth.*
>
> *It's time to go deeper*
> *into the wide horizons*
> *of practice.*
> *It's time to be*
> *what the wind calls*
> *us all to be.*
> *It's time to sing*
> *the song of the heart.*

I am Raven Now

April 6

Lo, I will be with you, even unto the end of the age.

Jesus

Early:

> I am the simple raven now.
> I am the darkness that glints in the sun.
> I am wings without thought of want.
> I am the need to be only flight and song.

Late:

> It is midnight.
> The wind chimes and ticking clock
> sing in time with my sleeping spouse and cat.
> The cabin is still and softly breathing.
> The click of the pen's talons fall upon the page,
> a rustle in the field of sheets.
> It is calm before the end,
> quiet before the beginning of the new world.

Meanwhile

April 11

The pen hovers and
then falls. A cloud
is bruising my eyes.
The world fades
into a night
dark with lightning.
Tired.
Scared.

Work has come
temporarily this week.
Tenderness is lost
with the savings
and the sawdust.

Meanwhile
the geese wheel north.
The body sinks
into the clay of this land.
The tides that cannot be owned
rise and fall.

Meanwhile
the field is pulsing.
The sap is rising.
The buds are bursting
with the ink of flowery snow.

Meanwhile
I'm opening up
as far as I can.
Who knows if the cloud
will fall with shocks of drizzle
or simply fly by
on its way to somewhere else.

On the Edge of the Field
April 12

Today the swallows
returned in spiraling flights.
I'd not seen them since their nests
failed in last year's deluge.

A coyote sat shyly at the edge
of the pasture, watching the farm slumber.
She, like the field, also
being a beautiful patchwork of quilted fur.

She trotted off into the dark woodland.
Then I heard a single gunshot yell out.
The swallows scattered like lightning.
I wonder if the coyote lives now?

Our world is so full of ruthless tenacity,
beauty and pain,
all mixed together in a storm.

The View From Here
April 15

My neighbor now stores his big white trash trailer right in the middle of my wide green view. It's just left, moldering in the middle of the field. Bright white and splashed with mud, upended. Doesn't anybody care for beauty anymore? Must I look at the white sore? Make it part of the landscape? Or see the whole? Or just take a different view?

Beauty is all around… the trailer too. This life is made of both shit haulers and dewy rye. We're all mud in the end, once shining and stored for a future of movement.

Last night I dreamt of earthquakes and tall buildings falling over with me and my beloved inside, tumbling upside down. I woke up to a jolt. I heard a rattle, a squeak of a trailer hitch. A shimmying of wheels for so long stilled.

Between Need and Desire
April 21

Before beginning anything else this morning, before the plans, the lists, the worries... Yet after making the kids breakfast, sending my spouse off to work, coddling the cat, feeding the chickens, emptying the bucket from last night's rain..... between the *need tos* and the *to-dos*... I will praise the world that is rising from the sunrise mist. This is a beautiful morning of fists uncurled and wild hair and drowsy garden. This memory will be the seed for sharing the produce of dung and clay and sweat and dreams. The early crops are bent in their final days, offering their glory to my singing knife and shovel, to end up on some happily burdened table, the bounty being consumed by so many people, becoming one with my customers, children and friends. The green ones offering themselves to the boiling pot and sweat lodge oven. Becoming more than themselves. These fruits and vegetables are the sun stored and then released in veins and breaths. This morning I praise the verdant field which offers its life for all who care enough to breathe. I choose the side of life that is filled with the once upon a time summer heat, with thirst slaked by the rain, with feet cooled in the loam and buried stone. Thank you Spirits of the Land for such bounty in between all the doings and undoings, in between the seasons growth and resting, in between inspiration and expiration.

Singing Last Night and This Morning

June 7

Last night the clouds and forest were
dancing at the edge
of the field.
This morning the sky lowered herself
in a curtsy, and cried
softly on the garden.

Until This Year

June 19

Until this year
I spent most of my mind time
being sentimental, attached
and swooning in dreams of someday.
Like my father, only soft.

How many days now
on this parcel
of rye and daisies?

How to be alive now,
rich in my poverty,
being flush in words,
deeds and the flowing
solvency of spirit?

Watching out the cabin
window for the first time in weeks.
I was bent on rearranging
the broken furniture
while gods walked out in the field.

Then I remembered pulverizing the altar
stone in the water of my youth and
then drinking it.
Taking the stone's essence
into the center of my being.
Ocean and Earth flowed.
This land is a part of me now too!

What am I if not free?
God in my heart.
God in the ink.
God even in the sentimentality.

I work in a garden of ruins.
Kneeling in muck of aloneness and
the walkway of constriction.

No longer a poet, or shaman or farmer.
Time for titles to wither.
I am only a man.
No longer a boy,
but a man,
out in the dirt
with the Beloved.

Beyond the islands that
swim within me,
flying past the sirens and gunshots,
the dogs and the dishes,
melting and rising,
breathing and dying,
I am a living song on the wind.

Sitting on the Front Porch on a Summer Morning
June 26

Reclined in the same low slung black canvas chair
that once sprawled in an island dream.
A dozen different birds sing up
the cloud's steamy memory of rain.
Shiva's name tumbles from the
crooked little speakers hanging
in the cob web of rafters.
The air is a luminous sultry sea.
The old familiar longing falls into
my shaking hand.
I awaken, here, tired from dreams
of rowing in circles
in the straits of fantasy.

Drums thrum in the background
of a tide surge song stream
illuminated by the rainfall.

I decide to truly be here:
I'll write the words given to me today.
I'll re-work the field of dirt and ideas.
I'll stack the wood for next winter.
I'll clear the closet's moth eaten shirts.
I'll plan for a last summer of freedom and constraint.

I work the land's binding seams,
sweating out
time's fickle fling of fate,
raising my gaze,
up from the black canvas,
through the clouds,
and into the sun.

Observing this Choreography
July 17

Perhaps I am the fool who is
not so foolish after all.

I am studying the rain,
perched at the cabin window again.

On the barbed wire fence
four fledgling swallows
shiver and wait. They watch
their parents swoop and dive
between raindrops, hunting
above the wild field.

How many wait out their scattered
lives without knowing
the essence of
this beauty?

Don't be so sure
you know what you think
you know.

We are only a moment
of breath, a lifting
of stars, a traipsing
of whispers between
the raindrops.

How can one survive
without observing
this choreography?

Is this both freedom and
madness to sit here all day
storing the experience
for eternity?

God's eyes are upon the field
of the living and the flying,
upon the rain and air dance,
while swallowing all of our tears and
singing to the burnished copper
of the sun.

What God Says When I am Afraid of the Future
July 18

This is your day.
Harvest your dreams.
Lay them up in a song.
Glean the garden's beauty.
Sit in the sun.
Make the difficult call.
Do not wait.
Move and commit.
Be still.
Sell the past.
Bank the future.
Be here.
Live in between.
Go out into life
and life will come into you.

Making a Medicine Wheel of Grass
July 21

I created a perfect circle within a circle of 180 feet in diameter in our pasture today. I cut and turned around the field in orbits. Mice ran in every direction from the scything blades, scattering to the four directions, creating a diaspora of a terrible joy. Then the twilight of swallow flight came down soft after the holy hum of the tractor went to sleep.

The next morning I look out on a patchwork of fields. Ours is the only field with a thousand birds spinning in circles. The grass is spiraling in the wind like the gyre of the great Pacific. This gyre sings praises for the world, a prayer to alleviate the suffering of our Mother.

The Spirit spoke from behind me:

This is what it is like when we work together.

I don't work hard this morning.
I did not work hard yesterday.
This is joy.
That was joy.

I was gliding and flying,
softly driving out
what no longer served,
praying in motion,
singing upon the deep
throated echo
of sea and sky,
floating in currents
of sweet grass.

Yogananda Comes to the Garden
August 22

The cat meanders around
the green and shiny rows of
beets and corn.
Then a bird flutters and
alights on a wire.
She freezes in perfect
concentration.
She pauses in
a vibrant tension
of stillness, fiercely
loving the one
of her desire.

Then the Master comes in the shimmer of corn leaves,
a soft whisper of God in sunlight
beside him. He smiles and says:

> *Be the cat in stillness*
> *with a focus of ardor and attention,*
> *being in love with your*
> *calling, purpose and delight.*

Planting the Orchard
September 1

Planting a tree requires faith.
Making an orchard enlivens a vision.

~~~

Last night I staked
the outline of the orchard,
in a series of perfect
squares and rows
which run diagonal
within the golden field's
wish for water.

Now I wait for the rain
to fall with the leaves.
The saplings wait
in their plastic buckets.
Soon enough it will be
planting time,
and we will all be
making a home for the future.

God's Promise to a Farmer Poet
September 6

You'll never have a regular job or regular success.
Believe it and the vision will grow.
You will be pushing your way
to the sun in continual re-formation.
(seed-leaf-flower-fruit-compost-seed)
You will be dead to the old ways
as much as the old is dead to you.
You are freely, uniquely
golden dirt for my planting,
my tending, my harvesting,
my care, my love.

I want one thing:
You,
in my field of starlight and mud.

The world of mortal greed is torn apart.
The world is being plowed
for planting and then harvest.
You are a seed among many seeds in my hand.

Take in the celebration as you are
scattered to the wind and earth.

Killing Wasps
September 29

I killed a hundred golden wasps
in a cloud of toxic spray.
Then I harvested a bushel
of grapes from their domain.
Once they were my allies.
Once they ate the other
insects that harmed our vineyard.

I wonder about the karma
of killing noble creatures so fierce.

I watched them die,
struggling in spasms.
Then I took their fruit
inside my home and
inside my body.

A Good Day to Die, A Good Day to Live
October 2

Redwing blackbird has returned
with the tree frog and robin.
Laced in the dew are hungry
slugs amongst the slain wasps.
The field is cut low in
rippling patterns of
last night's wind.
A distant rooster calls
to his laying hens,
all proud of their work.
Passing church traffic is whistling by,
rushing to find God
out there somewhere.
The bodies of the corn
stalks have given
their flesh as a sacrament
for our pleasure…Hallelujah.

Sitting on this bench
I observe my filthy pants.
I look down
at the tattered beard of white cotton
where my muddy boots pull
through the tired genes.

I think:
"These are the pants,
these are the thoughts,
these are the muddy verdant
memories I could be buried in."

A whole life could be lived
for just one moment
like this… or
like this… or
like this…
like this…

Passing into eternity's ticker,
I want to be worn out by summer,
like this field,
cut down by the wind.
Yet the stalk and chaff and seed
remain as part of the earth,
taken in whole fragments
to rise again come springtime.

Talking with Other Farmer's at the Grange Hall
October 4

Agenda - Weeds of tansy
     - Stream buffers
     - Glyophosphate
     - Flea beetles
     - Long summer days
     - Extravagant growth
     - Die back of the fodder
     - Gathering the seed corn
     - Sowing winter rye…
             oh, and:

           letting the wonder fall with the barometer,
           deep into the earth's core,
           deep into the interior of memory,
              the sower being the sown.

Sparring Sapsuckers
October 6

I.
Two Sapsucker's posture,
eye to eye,
in an ancient ritual
out beyond the garden fence.
Heads bobbing.
Squaring off.
Bodies swaying.
Corkscrewing flights
of frenzy.
Then stillness.

Fight or love-fest?
It's hard to tell.
No harm is inflicted
either way.
How fortunate
the animal world.

II.
The stories of praise
or blame we shed
within our star field
of thoughts are raging
fires, clearing and
crushing us into
crumbling shelters of spirit.
Remember the wide open mind.
The animal's field is our home too.

Clearing the Calendar
October 10

A whole day ahead.
Wide open,
like I've cleared
a field full of landmines and
revealed a flowered meadow again.

Summer is over.
The tick of the clock
is syncopated with
the rain in the downspout,
splashing out a reflection
of yesterday's drought,
dancing drops into the day ahead,
grateful to have traversed
this fire forged week.

Today: a ceasing, a resting,
propped up in the door way,
living on the threshold
of stewardship and purpose,
to be in-spoken instead of out.

Hands
November 7

I.

Last night in her field I watched her hands running through her long sunset hair. Her eyes laughing behind a picket of fingers. Then she reached out with a single finger and traced runes between my shoulders. We weave a web walking beside each other, with fingers crossing a boundary past fingers…the web that melts the winter frost. Her hands are long, delicate and capable of a stout load of work, washing and pleasure. Her hand upon my hand, rocks the cradle. Her finger sinks into the blue blood of this ink. Her wrist is kissed with the scent of grasses and dewy earth. Her hands are the world, the silken body of God.

II.

I look for the wisdom in hands. I see the lineage and the future in hands. I am a reader of palm, finger and vein. I know the truth of our greatest human instrument for death or life. God's toolbox, the hands. Even now these fingers are obeying the call for words. They are doing whatever is required to write the story of themselves and the lineage that courses in the bloodied rivers and secret canyons.

Instead of the faces, I see the hands of the dead and the breathing. The joy and wisdom in them, the fragility, the way they served and bent and wrote, their impact on my life. I look into the dark room of my mind and all I see are the hands.

Catching a Winter Chill
The Mole
December 14

I finally caught the ruffian mole.
She had created
a pile of perfectly
fertile soil excavated
with tenacity and wit.

The animal is dead now,
stuffed back into the tunnel
she once so skillfully dug.

And I am
alive for now,
digging my way
toward the surface
of light and danger.

Fifth Year

In the Garden
January 12

I have a beautiful dream
rising from within the darkest part of me.
I feel its gentle hand, warm upon my shoulder.
My world is safe at last.
The garden has overwhelmed the drought.
The sun shines but never burns.

Snow
January 18

I.
Solitary, but not
alone,
in the frozen field.
Soft mouth of snow
embracing the sky
of my eyes.

I know how
the blood courses
through my body now:
whoosh and pause,
a gentle tide layering
the silt of experience.

II.
In the heavy snow,
walking the bent
outline of last summer's
medicine wheel.

When I open my eyes
I see
my outline cast
upon the linen field.

A light shines
behind me,
around me,
flashing with
the watchers.

I remember what
the blood says to me,
how the blood sings
within me.

Brigit's Feast
February 1

Brigit,
be at peace with me.
You stand in our field.
Behold this pen in my hand.
What will I be now, my love?

You will plan and plant.
And what comes is determined
by the mood of the earth and air.

So be it.

I will
plant.
I will
write.

A Man is in the Field
April 5

A man is standing
in the field,
bent with snow.
The grasses asleep
in the crystal cold dark.

The man is pure white
with praise for the someday sun.

The man stands,
upright, shivering out
his sadness.

He knows the light
even in the dark
night of his heart.
He knows the day
will sometime shine
green and gold.
He knows the grass is
dreaming about bare feet
running in sunlight's carpet.

He is soaring
in the warm wind
coming from the sea.

Singing
May 7

The garden is singing.
The sun is singing.
The shadows in the woodland are singing.
I have another day here, on planet Earth!
I am singing.

List of a Good Day
May 10

Today:

- Repaired the tiller transmission
- Serviced the line trimmer
- Tilled clods into buttery seed beds
- Cut out the old peach orchard
- Planted a plum tree
- Made lunch and breakfast for the kids
- Went to the bank to make a deposit
- Picked up feed at the farm store
- Edged the tall grasses around the greenhouse
- Talked with kids about our personal dramas
- Wrote three times
- Spoke with mom about her health and mine
- Drove kids to and from school three times
- Read affirmations and then lived them
- Got the gentle slap of a sunburn
- Kissed my wife hello and goodbye and then hello again
- Heard a spirit whisper with glee: *Shazam!*

Stay. Fly.
Two Longings Fulfilled
May 15

One.

Harvesting Rhubarb.
Listening to hammers fall on the barn up the road.
The sun is rich and deep in the soil.
I am alone all day and in communion.
Working, digging a pipe trench up the hill.
Filling our house stores.
Finishing with hanging a full flag line of laundry in the dry heat.

Two.

In two days, leaving for my old home on the edge of an island.
This little farm to be left behind for that memory home.
I travel between in a rattling little trailer, like a sun bee to sunflowers.
I fly to the Salish Sea, looking across the sound.
Visiting the grave of my old lover.
My wife, the one I love now and forever, will wait for me.
I travel between the two in a shield of moon light and a disc of the sun.

The Poet's Job
May 19

Job Description:
> *To look out the window and see.*
> *To reach out to the world and show.*
> *To allow thought and memory to flow into the sea.*

The tide swept our flotsam and earth.
The sea ladled up the dreams unencumbered and unrehearsed.
The current is bound for the straits of the rocky pass and then out to open sea.
The sweet wrack fragrance is all that remains.

We are swimming in spirals of infinity,
sun warming the wind,
trying to heap the river back onto the land.
But the river cannot be stopped.
The moon and sun are
lovers repelled and attracted,
pulling up the threads of tides and weaving them into a blanket for their loving.
The thoughts of the river are melting into the straits.
The memories of a too little life are sinking into the open heart of the sea.

Rain of Shivers
June 3

A shiver of song rises up
as rain shimmies down my spine.
Garden is sown.
Water lines are connected
and set to flow someday.
Rain and wind rule today.
There is not much
to fret over that is
within my control.
The sky will always be
free and sacred.

Garden After the Hail
June 10

Perhaps the sun that filters through the mist will delight the field.
Perhaps the storms have returned to their mountain home.
Perhaps I will sit here with my wife and gaze a while longer.
Perhaps I will stop clinging to what could be someday and love what is.
Then I will thank the survivors and the faithful that inhabit the garden.

How Good, How Hard, How Right
After the Hail II
June 11

In the garden.
On the edge of fresh cut pasture.
Stretching limbs of unruly potato.
Elephant ears of primeval rhubarb.
Onions in ranks and rows.
Beans bent with dew.
Beaten squash trying to live free again
after their innocence was slashed with ice.

All alive because of You, Beloved.
I am here, alive too.
Make this being here my practice of Your presence.

How good this is.
How hard.
How right.

To My Farm
After a Long Trip
June 18

You went with me
faraway, into the mountains
where I was born.
You never left me.
You re-membered me back
from my childhood sadness.

My friend, my mentor, my lover, my brother, my child,
soil of my flesh, passing thought, manifest vision,
dirt of mole and root, sun-moon…
I am always home.

Samsara on the Farm
June 19

Yes, drizzle, I see you.
My old companion,
I feel you.

Heater pulses on at full bore
behind the pressing chill.
Slugs are moving in from all directions.
Farming is at a standstill,
at least on the surface.
Roots alive.
Tubers blossoming deep in the soil
where voles devour them,
churning the crop rows under
in their ecstasy.

All I can do,
is what I really wanted
to do all along:
write to you,
watch,
wander in
the sunlight of wonder.

I've had my head in the sun
most of my life.
Now it's as if a mist has fallen
in the summer season of my work.

I'll go deeper,
even as the naysayers and doomsayers
approach and uproot.
They come from every which way,
especially from within.

I tend the garden anyway.
Waiting.
Patient for the words.
Protecting the tender blossoms.
Free in the drizzle.
Grateful,
while all around the tamed are burning
in a climate change of forgetfulness,
a wildfire of inattention,
while here the green crops and
wondrous weeds are reaching
into the grey.

Growing Within the Rain
June 26

Cloud banks are crashing like the hordes
against the great serpentine wall
on the flanks of ancient China's mountains.
Here, the rain falls.
My hair falls.
The eyes of winter want
possession of summer.
But the air is still and sweet
between the corn rows.
The garden has burst
open with violet and gold and emerald.
It is summer and
we are growing within the rain,
not despite it.

Pre-Dawn
June 27

My body aches,
tired from the alarming snap
of my awakening.
My body is clean,
anticipating the tilling and the mud and
churning shit of field work.
The white sheeted surface of dreams
is crushed by the dark
universe of possibilities.
This ink filled page is a script
written for no one in particular.
These are jewels that will probably never
be seen in the light.

I'm not complaining,
at least not this early in the morning.
No.
My life is surprised by complications of joy,
the lonely responsibility of family and
the connection of a companion
who is also my wife.

Yes.
I am free,
tired,
a worn tine in the mud,
spinning in passion,
happy,
hopeful,
awake to every turn of fate.

In this place,
I make my stand,
beginning on my knees.
The earth of this place is
a part of me,
and I am part of it.

Truth Will Have Its Day
June 27

It's the sliver in the palm.
It's the chipped bone beneath the sock.
It's the grain of growth under the arm.
It's the black hole moving through the light of space.
It's the sickle in the green wheat.
It's the thought that is buried beneath all the long lists.

What am I telling?
Who am I fooling?
Someday the truth will have its day in the sun,
with the bones of my soul dried in the desert
where the field once swayed.
All will wisp away in the dust.

A simpler way is coming
said the Void.
A simpler way.

Making a Labyrinth of Mowed Grass
This is What is Holy
June 28

The field is a dewfall
of spiraling suns and shimmering moons.

But the magic is not in the visionary
borders between *this* or *that*, or
in the representation of the celestial, or
even in the work of imagination.

On the edges of the cuts
one can see the full living stalks,
from deep greens at the base,
to the vibration of gold in the swaying tops.
The pungent sweetness of the grass
shivers in the slightest breeze.
The cloud shadows dance in streams
across the face of the field.

The Earth itself,
                    this is what is
                              holy.

Who I Am Now
July 1

Cloud strewn body of memory.
Sun filled space of heart.
Ether spun with eternity's spirit.
Flesh of Earth.
Mind of God.

Thinking About Autumn
August 10

I keep thinking:
"It's the last
sunny day on earth."

Winter will come
and go.
Summer has
bowed down and
fall is shining
in the meadow.

I woke feeling
the bright sky gazing
through a tear in the rain;
the sun being my heart.

It's a good day.

Every day is a good day.

I'm a person of earth,
working in my own field and
singing a perfect
imperfection
with my friends.

Suddenly I'm not
thinking anymore.

Sixth Year

To the Descendants
March 26

If I had a time capsule to send to you:
I'd send this heady sweet spring sky full of pollen and birdsong and wild whispering clouds.
I'd send you this bouquet of the garden wrapped in my ragged wool sweater.
I'd send you this wind as it swiped and spun the fresh spring grasses in the field.
I'd send you this hint of loss and life, with death and desire held in my aging hands.
~
Can you sit awhile with me stranger?
I'm not so far away now.
Feel the heartbeat of the wind.
Know the thoughts of the dirt.
Catch the flickering wink of a song spun wing of the blackbird.
I am only on the periphery of your dreaming.
Sit a spell.
Wake me in you now.

I Once Only Wanted
April 16

Barefoot in the tall grass,
beneath the family tree
where we were wed.
I hold the trunk,
caress the bark,
listen to the swaying
chimes in the branches.
Leaves are making love
with the fluttering sky.
Roots are held, so strong and tender,
within the earth.
One tree brings the world together.
How good it is to renew vows every day.

I once only wanted a legacy.
Now, I want to be happy and free,
a forester of song,
a farmer of words,
a father of the loved,
a faithful failure who was
lost and then found on this planet,
in this garden, within this home.

Perhaps Grateful Grief
April 18

I want to make a beautiful
impact today.
So many seeds to offer
to the willing earth.

Last night I dreamt
of crying and crying,
unceasing crying.

And I felt
relief
in the storm.
Perhaps grateful grief is my
gift today, nourishing
the garden and my dreams.

Death Day
I Remember I Don't Remember
April 19

I Remember Now:
I am not the chaos any more than the sun is the rain in my head.
My head is full of memories.
But many of them are sidelined by sad and sweet stories.
I remember Jupiter last night shining and flickering and singing to the blackness,
shattering my reflections of pain.
I push away the injustice of our world, the yelling, the smirking, the petulance and the….
oh, I just want to remember Jupiter rising with the moon.

I Don't Remember:
because I wasn't there.
I blacked out when you touched me.
I became a root rotten in the mud.
Oh, I can't, I won't…
but my very cells remember
and that fills my body with escape tactics.
So much worrying lives in my head that soap would never make me clean.
Back then I forgot all about the magical tricks of light.
O, I will recall Jupiter from last night.
Mother, Father, God is One.

I Remember on My Death Day:
writing in the cabin window,
making lovely eyes with my wife in the little yellow trailer,
the tears when I finally sold a thousand books.
I was so happy I danced in the field.
O, that field, so full of grasses bent in the headiness of fall.
I remember a wild tangled island and her sweet waft of tides,
how God always accompanied me to the other side of the straits.
I remember breath.
I remember the drum signing me home.
                    Now I am home forever.

In the Garden II
April 21

In the Garden:

    Mist.
    Cool mud.
    Coastal fog.
    Bird song.
    Wild rhubarb
    and collard and strawberry.
    Working so hard
    I both hurt and smile.

Hear the creek singing?
Like it has for ten thousand years.
See the robin hunt,
her quizzical look,
swaying side to side?

She has come home
to this round verdance.
Like me.
Stalking the physical,
the meat of the real,
where the joy begins.
My tired muscles sing:
        loam of Om
        loam of sky
        loam of wonder

The Desk, The Window, The Heart
May 17

Considering the Desk

Once it was only a place to write and dream.
Now it is a platform to reach out into the world,
to not be alone in my connection, and
to marvel over the meaning of love.

Considering What is Outside My Window and Inside My Heart

The farm shudders with growth.
We live in a verdant poverty.
But I have this desk, this pen, this prayer:

God, work through me and love me
beyond sense and logic and even pleasure.
Be my partner and lover,
here on this page, my refuge and light.

Kali of the Rain

May 18

Kali: The goddess who slashes the illusion that we are only our bodies.
She brings death of the ego. Sometimes her lessons can appear harsh.
But her intention is the liberation of the soul.

A season too cold for the seedlings to come up.
Bugs and voles and fungus move in anyway,
waiting for their turn at the coming feast.
For every act of creation there is an echo of Kali.
This is not just destruction,
but an assemblage of lovers,
an offering from the universe,
to the universe.

As a gardener,
my protective efforts must be
carried out with humility and honor.
Me, being a son of Kali too.

Beginning and Ending

Just Begin Again and Again

May 20

In the Morning

The necessities of effort
are dense with labor and time.
How do I
make a farm,
create a business,
care for children,
be a husband and
write with my spirit friends?

Just begin.
The ending is assured.
Form and fate are fluidic.
Our good work is
the sun illuminating
our verdant ocean of love.

In the Evening

Long labor.
All day in the sun,
blazing with effort that is
no effort at all,
remembering the clods cut
into new earth,
and the sculpted concentric rings
of the field's finery.

Breakfast
May 28

A bowl of cinnamon, wheat and cold milk.
Warm cream in dark coffee.
Adding another bowl and cup
to the altar of my ancestors.
We sip in silence.
Together.

A candle sings to our dreaming.
All moments have come to this.
All moments will flow from this.

Weeding
May 28

A day of digging and tilling lies ahead.
A day of pulling out the weaker shoots,
with the strong and lucky ones remaining.
All destined for sun,
yet reaching into the rain.

Becoming a Child Again
May 29

Unless you become like a little child you cannot enter the kingdom of God.
Jesus

I am not old now.
I am not young,
except in my heart.
I am autumn in a summer shimmering with heat,
rising into thoughts like lightening.
I am a-live,
giving all of myself in service.

Please be *Kindness*
in my temple,
Sweet God Almighty,
Lover,
Keeper of my fire,
Flooder of my verdant field.

How Many Days Like This?
May 29

Heavy Rain:
> Sheets cast off by lovers in heaven.
> Blue-green sprouts in the field
> drowning in kisses.
> Sugared caresses of sky song and
> earnest sun-fall trying to reach
> into their roots.

This Body:
> My temple of the Beloved,
> inundated by the years
> within the silken sun.

This Incarnation:
> I am springtime warmth in autumn.
> I am sacred mud drowning with life.
> I am free to work
> my way into the ground,
> roots searching into life,
> wet with life's fires.

Holy, This Chance to Live
June 8

Garden Verdant.
Bills mostly paid.
Breeze wafting the salt from the horizon's distant ocean.
Seeds awakening from the dark places.
Holy, this opportunity to live.
Holy, this day.
Holy, this chance to breathe in the sun.

Building the Greenhouse
June 12

Unfurling brightness,
erecting the gothic arches,
lifting our arms in the rain.
The greenhouse is rising,
a shelter from the rain
within the rain.

Early Season Garden Prayer
June 15

My Song to the Seedlings:

Grow now in summer.
Grow now in deep soil darkness.
Grow now in mystery of what weather will come.
Arriving, I wait.
Planning, I work.

God's Reply:

All will end and live forever.
What you add here is added to the whole universe.
What you take away will be remembered in the great healing.

Bounty
May 14

The list of to-dos today:

> paint
> till
> weed
> promote
> serve
> call
> drive
> weed again

Setting the list down I ask:
"What does it mean to live?"

Ah, the sun and the passing
shades of clouds
dancing through the trees,
I hear your reply.

We are here for a moment
of good sweet difficulty.

We work the ground
of attending.

Do you hear the robin sing gaily?
I am that bird.
I am only a moment
of song in the field
of waves and light.

God, What is Our Agenda Today?
June 25

Remember the tree you beheld in the swaying field.
Remember the fairy lights you danced with in the midnight forest.
Remember our daughter so free in the desert, singing up the sun.
You are of these.
You are free.
You are loved.
Be the image of the imageless, wearing gender only as a raiment.
Be the shining one, being both bright and fragile.
Be the flowers that bloom and are never cut.

I Want Everything
July 15

I want green islands,
bursting garden,
happy people.
To own them, I cannot.
I want the whisper of Raven's sea,
humming of Raven's sacred garden,
laughing of Raven's tribe.
To have these now, I have not.

What are you willing to give to me, God?
What am I willing to offer for your callings,
and for your responses,
so gentle and severe?

Everything.

New Earth
July 17

A mist hovers over the cabin.
The field is brown, with grasses bent like an army of monks in prayer.
Outside the window, I recognize the new earth.
The old ideas are healed, renewed and vibrant with possibility.
Inside, I sit bent over my desk.
My desk is the friend I fashioned with my own hands,
but only after the grain ripened in the rings of sun circles and forest song long ago.
Me and this desk, both from the wild,
cut down, remade, refined for a time,
awaiting renewal…O Sacred Earth, renewal.

Longing in the Middle of Farm Season
July 20

I long
to dive into your thighs,
your hands grabbing my hair and
reaching into my back,
then tearing out my lungs
along with my heart.
You take my breath away and then give if back to me.
You are my beloved in unexpected winter warmth.
You are the lover in salty sprays.
You are the high moan of raucous seas.
You are the chorus in the swirling clouds.
You are all names and all wonders.

Please write your song upon my heart.

Reading the Poems Beside the Open Window
August 10

I see the stitching
so finely woven through
the binding of the book.
I see the field and its cat
stalking her mouse.
I see the glass reflecting
the white page and
the steam of coffee.

I lift the page,
praying to the one
who is me and
not me.
I lift the weathered
handwriting into rainbows
of ocean spray.
I lift the heart into the blue white sky,
into a spaciousness
married to the waves.

Isn't that how it is?
We look at one thing and
see another?
Yet life is not just a metaphor
for the hidden and the hiding.
Heaven and hell are
all around us.

So, I choose Heaven,
as hell has made me
hungry and seeking
after beauty and grace and
all that is right
with the world...
all that already is.

Farmer Who Lives Half Way Up the Mountain
Alpenglow on Silver Star Mountain
August 1

I live half way up the mountain.
I see both the heights and the valley
when not obscured
by the forest of dreams and
sentiment and all manner
of tangled thoughts.

Caught up or
enthralled, I work
my fields and
tend my orchard.
Simple tasks
turn through my heart until
I am tilled, sprouted and
harvested, then tilled
again and again.

Am I free?
Truly?
O Mountain,
where do you reside and
what do you know?

Not only the clouds and sun,
but the very molten heart
of the earth I know.

And I know you, human.
And soon you will be
a part of me.

Nellie
August 16

While working at the farmer's market.

I became a farmer yesterday at 6:35 PM as the sun settled within the dust in the wide trampled field of our tents. I'd offered smile after smile until all our produce was gone. The vegetable gifts were disseminated across the wide wandering earth, to become flesh and bones and dreams. As I was tearing the tent down a fellow farmer approached me. A woman in dusty braids looked into my harvest of emptiness and said "You are so very kind." Then she simply walked away.

She had bestowed a holy benediction. What I had to offer was really only love made manifest. After all the weeding, busting clods, chasing rabbits and cutting succulent green stalks, I came and sold all I had. When I had nothing left I offered the only thing that is no thing. And it came back to be reincarnated in a kind recognition by a fellow soul.

We give and give and give.
And when we are empty, we offer up the real harvest.
And so we become farmer-lover for a moment.
And that moment is forever.

Not Vahalla
Old Norse Valhöll: *The Glorious Hall of the Slain*
August 19

Steeped again with *here.*
Afraid I won't ever write
of beauty again.
This is the tyranny
of the enlightened:
Once visiting Valhalla,
then coming back
to Middle Earth,
we rarely return
to the fields
of the gods.
And longing prevails
for a long season.

What now, Spirit?

Write
of the trash dancing
in the summer gusts,
or the forge of forests
reborn in fountains
of flame.
Write of the
sadness that comes
with love.
Write of God's
beautiful tears
shed daily
over all this planet.
This is good enough,
this is god enough.

Slugs
September 5

I slink, stealthy,
into the cool wet garden,
murder on my mind.
Old shears jawing
the death song
in my right hand,
warm casual coffee
in my left.

"This is your last day on earth."
I tell each one slithering
toward an unrequited delight.
Then I fall from the sky.
Then I cut the life force free.
Then I become Death.

Death, hovers over me too,
her sharp songs
in her dripping blade.
Her casual saunter,
her fierce mission
to soon free me
from my earth bound delights.

These are your last
moments on earth,
she will say.
Soon you will awaken.
Soon you will be free.

While Visiting the City
From a Beaten Country
September 6

How does the soft place attract a hard fear?
How does the asphalt attract earth lovers and healers?

Where I live one must be hard in a soft place.
Here, it is soft in a hard place.

Where I live the big trucks tailgate.
Here, the bicycles congregate.

Where I live the land sings and sighs beneath
        the whirling slash of the mower's blades.
Here, the pavement smothers the earth
        while the trees stretch heavenward, unmolested.

Where I live "I've got mine." is "Hallelujah!"
Here, they say "We're in this shit together."

Where I live the neighbor's dog is chained to a post
        in the middle of a wide rolling field.
Here, the kids run with their pets
        on a land that is beaten down and hard.

Where do I live?
That is a mystery.

Moving Into the Beaten Country

September 6

Part One

Can I feel safe anywhere on my earth?
Where is the bright space between darkness and darkness?

> *Blow the embers of love.*
> *Light the blaze of truth.*
> *Be in right live-ly-hood.*
> *Cling to nothing here.*
> *The barking and the baby's cries are fire, fire, fire.*
> *Burn with me.*

Part Two

Odin cut out one eye so he could see in the darkness.
He saw angel songs and he seized them and then gave them away to everyone.
He saw the green molested earth as a witness to everything.

Odin had one eye in each world.
One experience,
two views.
One death,
two lives.
Me,
Thou,
God,
All.

What little fear would I kill to sing and laugh?
What grief would I face to live God's love?

A Farmer's Questions
September 12

What crop is the highest good for me, the earth, and the people?
Is it only food I grow?
What do we really make here?
Is this tilled earth exalted, then demeaned, or is it partner and beloved?
Moles, voles, fungi, beetles, are these enemy?
Is there any honorable way to call one "Adversary"?
Am I akin to a god here, deciding how to plant and where to kill?
Am I also like a god, frustrated with what the little people do?
Or am I just another furrow awaiting my turn for water, the hoe or the knife?
What is this work for, God?
And who am I here?

Just Be a Yourself, Not Matter What
September 15

Anyway a poet can make living is acceptable.
Be a poet though,
not the self-referential sentimental one,
not the one who is "called",
not the redneck with naysayers creeping into your reptilian brain,
not the arrived householder who spiritualizes every turn of words.

Just be one who writes,
Just be one who shows what is there
in the plain glory of words.

As a famer I am mostly failure, so far.
I just tilled under an entire field of withered crops.
Fruitless, if I'm just a farmer.
Everything is food for the lover.

Last Farmer's Market of the Season
September 27

A day
of ruffling banners,
rolling white clouds,
air chilled and bright.
I had a moment talking with friends and customers that
I knew flowed within the marriage of joy and purpose.
Like art or harvesting or a moment of lovemaking
when you lose the *you* of thought and memory and
simply become the grateful god of now.

Storm Mind Storm
September 28

Tails of a cyclone throw their energy
into whipping the forest,
breaking the corn stalks,
slanting rain from the north,
and slashing from the south,
all at the same time.
Powerful.
Untamed.

I go out to the garden,
drain the pipes and put up the hoses.
I wash the carts and scrape the truck,
fold the towels,
look at the phone for messages while
the spirits laugh in the wind.
They shout:
> *Foolish man.*
> *Have you forgotten*
> *your first wondrous love?*

All my efforts and thoughts
spin me from far away.
I have made a storm
slanting from every direction
but one,
the one within.

So, here I am God and Spirits.
Thou and my Beloveds,
in the tempest.
Here I am
in the whipping taunts
of my little storm.
It's already late,
but here I am.

Owl Song
Awake Before the Light
November 4

Turned off the music.
Unplugged the heater.
Switched off the light.
Waited for traffic to calm in my head.
Set the coffee down.
Listened.

An owl sings her brilliant
love song in the dark,
chanting death and longing
above the chicken coop.

Together in the dark,
the singer and the sung to.
All we have is this lovely
melody from the shadows
that even night could not
overwhelm.

All the noise,
the damned
distracting noise,
will return
one switch at a time.

Yet, someday the power
will trip and stumble and
the sun will fall
for the very last time.
Then, that song,
the one that is sheltered from the light,
will rise in a voice singing:
who who who.

Then, those once hidden eyes
will turn and look
deep into me, and
deep into you.

Vulnerability
November 4

The greenhouse has only a paper thin covering of plastic creating its own climate.

Tobacco, peppers, eggplant
blossom in the hall of light.
Corn tassels hang fragrant.
Soil rises up in sweet perfume.
It's winter
and
it's spring,
with only a
thin veil
between
the two.

Home
November 13

Home:
Ho--
--Me
-Om-

Spring is coming:
   Hands in the dirt.
   Hands pulling wild geraniums.
   Hands uncovering the infant shoots of next year's garlic.
   Hands reveling in the young radiance of an aging life.

Summer is coming:
   Clay in the fingernails.
   Clay in the bones.
   Clay in the clothes.
   Clay sinking into the pores.
   Clay nourishing the seedlings.

Fall is coming:
   Growing inward.
   Growing downward.
   Growing toward the hidden disc of the new moon.

Winter is coming:
   Garden dreaming in a frosted arc.
   Garden dreaming in a slashing gale.
   Garden dreaming in cycles of star and storm.
   Garden surrendering to the stream of gravity,
      which pulls everything toward its source.

Crazy
December 3

Sun on the frost.
Trees punctuating the inky dome of sky.
Blue pen on the white page.
Soul already stumbling out on the front porch,
      drunk on awe, crazy in love.

Ordinary Wonder
December 14

The mist lies upon the land, a blanket of grace and quietude. I am listening to a haunting song of essraj and guitar. The coffee is silken warmth. My journal is spread out. The pages are white and simple like the field outside the window. I write. Whatever comes, I write.

Then I'm called out of the room. Just for a moment. A change.

Coming back. Sitting down. Same coffee. Same music. Same scrim of fog outside. But a new moment. The old is gone. The old inspiration, the old story being carefully scribed, then tucked away. The sweet old way of thinking, the sense of flow gone. And I sit, blank. Blank as the grey winter. A little bewildered. What can I expect? Everything changes. The old reverie morphs into a new question. After five decades I am learning this cycle of creation over and over again.

Yet.

Sometimes I long for how it was. Long for the coffee and the music to soothe like it did before coming back to a messed up home in a new moment. I long for the flood upon the page. I long for the happiness of a sad song. I long for the bliss.

Looking toward my short horizon, I see the field. In and out the mist dances, slinking and snaking through the forest. The window frames grey and deep shadows from a hidden sun. Soon enough the sun will come forward. Someday the forest will fall and rise and burn. Or some other calamity arising from ordinary beauty will arrive. The years have taught me to surrender to a new experience again and again.

We are wind gusts, passing through this life, passing through these mists and occasional clarities.

Moment by moment, what remains?
Who is experiencing this grace of being alive?

What would life be if we could answer these two seemingly simple questions?

Perhaps we'd be free to roam through time.
Perhaps we'd be free of the leaving everything behind as the next moment comes.
Perhaps we'd be free to peer through the fog.

But for now, I try and reach to you, Beloved. Through the electrons on the page and the weavings of space and time, satellite to Earth, through the cable and into your flickering screen. Now, this moment shared with you is not so ordinary anymore.

Translation of the Winter Garden
December 15

This is the experience:

> The flowered fragrance of winter clay,
> a granite perfume,
> a wafting string of ice,
> a water well of burnt offerings,
> bent and melted kale,
> rusty wire coiled with care,
> a broken fence post,
> another year flooded and then blown away,
> the new season rising,
> ready or not.

This is the translation:

> I can no longer resent or
> hate those that God wove
> into this universe.
> Even if they hate
> with cynical minds.
> Hate only grows
> with hate applied.
> It is either all God or none.
>
> I am made as I am,
> to grow through the winter of my life
> toward an end unknown.

Seventh Year

Genesis
Setting Arches Over the Garden Gate
January 16

He set a knotted arch over the entrance to his someday garden.
The arches were lower than the man's head and higher than his aspirations.
His creation being both humbling and edifying.
A small red sparrow lit upon his rugged cross.
The workman smiled at the feathered benediction.
"It is good." he said on the end of the sixth day.
And on the seventh day he rested.

Three Ways to Live in the Garden
January 17

One	Two	Three
Third Person	First Person	Second Person
To talk about	To speak at	To communicate with
Materialistic	Dogmatic-religious	Shamanic
In the particular	Summing up	The whole
Chance	Fate	Co-creation
You	Me	Me and Thee

January 18

Why can't I let the dog be silent when it's silent outside?
Why do I actually seek the noise when it either barks in my head or barks out there?
It's calm right now, why is there ruckus between my ears?
What say you, Spirits?

Spirits:

> *The sun is falling in thy spirit home.*
> *Our voices are the disturbing ones.*
> *Ready, set, disintegrate.*
> *We're the loving destroyers that you…You…called here into being.*
> *How is it to really live?*
> *Would you really know?*
>
> *When you lust after wants, what occurs to your soul's calling, its deep longing?*
> *Your heart withers in the onslaught of disturbance.*
>
> *Protect what is holy.*
> *Sanctuary for the spirit is in the walls of open sky.*
> *Make this place your own while breathing it in and out.*
> *Don't reign destruction inside your garden.*

God, I feel vexed, obsessed, suppressed.
I curtail my farm work to avoid the sound assaults of dogs.
How do I approach this with a plan for peace?

God:

> *Be Peace! Every bark is a moan of the universe.*

How do I live without fear?

> *Move out and protect your home with an open sky heart, yet fenced mind.*
> *Fence it: Talk it out.*
> *When calm in spirit, co-create silence and beauty.*
> *See what is right and incorrect.*
> *The dog is not beside you, is she?*
> *No, she is a hundred years away.*
> *Every bark is a call to silence through song.*
> *Fake it, if you must.*
> *Create, pray, love, respond…*
> *These are your vows,*
> *which the dog sings to you.*

Torn Up in Mid-Winter
Hurt Back, Injured Knee, Torn Diaphragm
February 8

Heavy snowfall and ice.
I slipped with unsure footing and tore a deep muscle in my inspiration.
My diaphragm was left burning and quivering after the fall.
The ragged edge of pain borne from assisting a neighbor in need.
I dug out her car, receiving a hug and a smile.
Now the snow tumbles off the roof.
Now I am stuck in my quaint cabin
writing to you from within a broken body.
Writing to you beloveds, dear ones, God,
reader unknown, my family deceased,
my daughter lost in the storm.

So much labor lies ahead of me this year.
Yet my body may betray my long list
of haves, musts and needs.

What if I could write the truth to you
in my convalescence, like this?
What if being was the only work I could do?
What if I could be the artist
in residence on a snow sodden farm?

The snow falls,
burying the earth I am to tend.
Let it fall.
Let it smother all my little plans.
Let the earth sing blood red love songs deep in my chest.
Let me write these words and then bury them,
waiting for the light of spring.
                                                    ~ ~~
Bury me:
        I'm ready to die.
        I'm ready to live.
        I'm ready for your ruthless wounding hand.
        I'm ready to do all that I could not do.
        I'm ready for the snowfall in spring.
        I'm ready for snowfall through summer.
        I'm ready for the colors to bloom in my head.
        I am writing my readiness into my flesh.
        I am raising the sun into the cold flutter of a white world.

In the Age of Dithering
February 19

Love, how did we end up here?
In the country
of stuffed houses that never laugh,
in kitchens with empty kettles that never whistle,
beside rooms of unblinking eyes staring at flickering screens,
full of empty in the dark.
I'm too old to raise children
addicted to lies.
I am too soft for the wonder of sales and
consuming all that is not real, true or compassionate.

How did we end up here,
swinging the sickle into the bent promises of a brittle field,
with only the throaty song of lawn mowers to soothe us?

Here we are on earth as it is in heaven,
in this age of dithering
while our planet sputters
into flames.

Four Snippets of Song in a Day
February 19

1.
So much to do in the field
now that the barking dog has
retired to her inner pastures.
Listen here.
Listen there.
Makes no difference.
Might as well work.

2.
The second night
in our shared bed.
I am drugged for sleep.
But I need no drug for love.
I love you
with every breath,
sleeping or waking,
tangled, tossing or enraptured by dreams,
I love you the same.

3.
These are the songs
no one will hear
but you, Beloved.
Listen,
be my scribe and
I'll be your fool.

4.
Be the witness
of what others
may not see.
Then tell them.

If I Were to Die Today at 6 PM
February 23

If I...
the awareness I call *I*...
were to leave all of this today, say at 6 PM, what would I savor?
What would I miss come sunrise the next day?

For one thing, watching my wife.
Like right now she is walking in the field below me, breathing in the silence.
Or watching her work on stitching prayer flags, so intent, content.

How about the feeling of warm sheets this morning?
Or the warm loam falling through my open fingers?
My fingers.

The white of this page and smooth skin of its body waiting for these words to fall right here.
Or the singing in a circle of drums.
Hearing the whoosh of a raven's wings in the rocky headland forest.
Then there are the tears of meeting my friend's loving gaze.

Salt spray from the sea, I'd miss that.
Leaving on a trip early in the morning before light has touched the silver starred mountain.
Laying in the waving grasses with my beloved.
I think I'll go down and meet her in the field.

The list is my life. The list meanders and grows with each day on earth. Holy, this life, holy.
Don't forget it. Do you see it? Do you recognize the miracle of what is breezing through our
awareness, and the sad beauty of what just slips by, unseen, unknown, uncelebrated?

I celebrate today, while it is today.
How about you?

To the Writing Desk After Working
February 24

275 trees were stuffed
into the back of my truck.
Then I planted their bare roots,
so full of life.

I should have come here first,
before I spent myself
on shovel work.

As it is, I can barely manage my life
without you, my inner creation.
I am a load of roots
upside down and
scribing in mid-air.

Yes, I needed to plant those trees today.

But, from now on let's keep
first things first.

To dig deep
one must become dirty,
sometimes becoming mired in mud.
The day in the clay has ended.
Here I am,
with nothing much to say,
writing all my nothings
to you.

What Happens While Walking

Between the House and the Cabin
February 26

Sometimes I think,
then I think better.
Between the house and the cabin I meander.
This is the beauty time of day.
My thoughts rise out
of the figuring and worrying.
I think fuller when inhabiting my body.
Then for a moment
I don't think at all,
like a child wobbling off
his training wheels,
his bicycle rolling free for moments
before he touches down again
upon his orbits of support.
Now I'll remember
the rolling free
all day long.
I'll remember all
the possibilities of freedom.

The Wind Said: *Sit, Watch, Listen*
March 7

Sit, watch, listen.

What is there to do today, but
sit-watch-listen?

Your job on Earth is to
see,
feel,
smell,
sense,
hear.

O, there are the friends and
cats and children to fawn over.
But in your heart,
you know your job on
earth is just
to notice what others paste
over with their activity,
pushing, digging, wringing
their way into the light.

Will you know the Earth
before you become Her
once again?
What good is the worship
of to-dos?
What path has anyone,
if not in this waking dream?

Monk Gardener
March 8

No one on earth will read these things.
I am alone with you
in a cell in my mind.
Is this heaven or hell or
something else altogether?

I tenderly transcribed
twenty poems this week.
I filed them away
beside the many boxes
of books and notes
that no one buys,
no one sees,
no one loves,
but you.

Feeling small sorrow for myself.
I'm the priest of sadness today,
another voice in a wilderness,
Dusty John,
baptizer of voles,
confessor of asparagus.

I painted another beautiful
flower for you, God.
Take it.
I give all I have to you.
Take me and my words,
that you may love
the garden inside of me
with your sweet smile.

Ancestors,
read my work.
I am the culmination
of all your yearnings.
Here I am.
Give me to the world,
as a dusty offering,
a ragged sacrifice,
a cell mate of God.

On the Edge of the Storm
Abundance
March 8

Rain pauses.
Quiet for now,
except for the tinkling
of the downspout pouring itself out.

Farming is a wonder
of waiting and wanting,
loving what is left between
storm and sun and ooze of clay.

I Must Tell You
Ghost Reader
March 11

Why do I write here?
Why do I transcribe
the thoughts
of an aging soul every day?
What use?
The answer is mystery.
But one glimmering resonates:
I must create or die!

What about you,
ghost reader
of an uncertain future?

Do you live
as you must,
even if it is lonely
out there in
your wide open field?

Here I am
writing to you again:
I love you, reader,
I Love You!
I must tell you
in a thousand ways.

Nothing Writes Nothing
Remembering Robert
March 17

Nothing to write?
Then write about nothing.

The robin sings brilliantly
in the clean sunshine morning.
But I listen for the dog barking, anyway.
The desk is piled up.
The to-do list is dense.
The dreams that woke me up this morning
sleep, forgetting themselves
in the mud of the garden.
And the cat and I sit and listen for them,
one of us for the birdsong,
one of us for the fears.

All day I think of my friend who died,
how life condenses
into a few crystalline moments.
In his case, a few moments in the sun and
meadows of the high juniper hill.
All the nothings bloom in the
forgetting of detail after detail.
Memory condenses
like a haiku wadded up on the desk.

Events seem to be lost,
but a few remain as gems
of afterthought,
diamonds from the pressure
buried deep in the earth.
My dreams are alive
for now
until they melt
into the
mud
too.

Dialogue with Time
April 2

Time, the motivator, the tormentor, the one loving us all into *The Presence*, I feel your hand pressing upon my shoulder. And I cannot tell if you are an insistent lover or a ruthless thug. What do you want from me?

To keep your word and be enlivened by living the wonder you write to me.

Is there any titled life that could satisfy me?

Sooner rather than later you will need to choose one.
And you already know which one.
You know the path you would regret not taking.

What should I do with all I am dreaming here with you?

Plant it all and give it away. Sell it. Consume it. Celebrate it…Life.
Make a splash as you dive into the cosmic ocean.

Words…more words. Am I a farmer of words, harvester of color, sower of beauty and truth?

Show, don't tell.

Restringing the Old Healing Drum

Letter to J after Nine Years
April 4

Hello Friend,

I had a dream last night. All our friends were there, the living and the dead. We moved and danced in a circle. Nine times we passed around the altar. Then facing each other, we turned another nine times. It's been nine years since I saw you in a living circle. Nine times around the sun, nine times you have been the sun.

My friend, where have you gone? Or was it me that transfigured and became speechless and mutely shining in the dark?

Yesterday I restrung the healing drum we made together. Even after stringing it, it still sounded limp and tired. Maybe it just needed more time in the heat and the light. Maybe it just needed another nine years. In nine more I'll be preparing for that little cabin on the dark hill too. Maybe I'll be in a dry season in the desert and thunder will bring that round rolling song back to life. I'm grateful for the effort to string up another tune, even if it is only the rain that sings.

I'll dance anyway. Befuddled by the strange shuffling steps of you who have gone ahead. I'm alive and I am trying to learn what you taught me. But my feet seem to stumble and stare from their caves of leather and lace.

Pretty soon I'll have to remember and tell the truth: I am not alone with my muse. I am her. And maybe that's why I can't see her, feel her, know her out there… because she's not out there, at least not for the past nine years.

If I can't play the happy song anymore, what about the joyful? I still barely hear the drum of our circle. Do you hear it? No wonder the old frame and skin is flat, the rhythm is buried in the soul, within a barely lit room full of sputtering candles with no ceiling, open to the wide and starry sky.

The song is still real. You are still real, as real as the island currents whooshing in and out of my heart, as real as the farm of weeds and wonder, as real as the little village in the foghorn of early morning, as real as *this* word. Words, one after the other. Words, shuffling in a circle of drums. Words making me dance past what I'd forgotten. Words that brought me home to a life that was never mine alone.

Pretty Soon
April 4

Pretty soon I'll have to choose again to winnow down what I pursue. Life is obviously no longer about being in perfection or even service. I'm tired and still breathing. What if I just kept on writing, not just stopping after the first climax of insight? Just kept at it, went past the boundaries of time and even grace? What if I got messy, unruly, and selfish in my love for you? What if I went into discomfort and then came back out again and wrote the truth unaltered? Not the pretty truth, but the weedy garden full of hungry rabbits and fermenting fruit jumbled up in wild happiness?

At the Farm Expo
April 5

I know how to:

> Raise the pH so the roots will uptake the earth's nutrients.
> Be careful not to burn the tender shoots.
> Use pilled calcium on the fallow fields.

I was surprised by how:

> The tingle came in the broadcasting of lime.
> You were there with green and scorching eyes.
> Your hands laced like roots with fixations on nitrogen.

I forgot the dreams of dust and weeds, and then:

> You grew up my spine and sprouted in my mind.
> You blossomed pistols of wonder in crimson red and sulphur yellow.
> I learned your simple formula: *Just raise the vibration and sweeten the soil.*

Who's Musing Here?
April 11

The power of solar streams are rushing into the void.
But it is no void, just the grey of all potentialities.
The *bardo*, they say.
What is this power that illuminates all from within,
so that the illusion of sun and field and sky and stars shine *out there*?
It is the unnamable,
the *I Am that I Am.*

What if we were all really melting
into a dark formless death?
Is that not
the eternal fear of all mankind?
Is that fear not the curse of the expulsion from the garden?
Melting into what?
The bardo?
Wouldn't that make us the everything of God's gaze,
turning us into everything that we already are?

Who's musing here?
And to whom is it mused?
I don't know.
I just send the sun streams into the wet dark void
and watch what grows out of that giving.

Mixed Up
April 18

I live.
I live in the most fertile land.
I sometimes live in dissatisfaction.
I died in such, once.
I live now from that point with acceptance and celebration.
I plant, though the seedlings are eaten.
I plant again with hope after the way it is.
I live between a struggle to survive and a celebration of fate.
I live in the loss of someday.
I am animated until I am everything.

Pests
April 24

What a familiar surprise every time creatures swarm in to partake of the garden's bounty. Though I should not be so surprised. Slug to chard. Vole to beet. Rabbit to lettuce and cabbage. Sparrow to seed and seedling. Aphid to stem. Flea beetle to leaf. Stink bug to everything else.

"Don't take this ravaging so personally", I say to myself. This is the way of the world. Life brings on life. Food attracts the hungry. It's not personal. Rather it's a perfect balance. Perhaps the plants that died were not strong enough, not tended with care, tended with too much care, not resolute in the genetic make-up, not lucky enough. Perhaps there are no reasons. Like anywhere there is light in the world, shadows bloom too. The trick is to be at peace with the way it is, not resisting it, not railing against anything that is true to its own nature. Yes, protect the garden you love. Envision its bounty as a goodness for the world, including the people and the bugs.

The Little Rabbit Takes a Bite Out of My Confidence
April 24

I caught the marauding rabbit in the spring loaded cage. He had been wiping out rows of vegetables that I'd carefully sowed in the garden. Lost harvests he caused me. I let him go on the other side of the swinging gate. Only a fence line away, I released him, knowing that all paths lead back to the garden home. Was this mercy? Maybe it was just recognition. The Spirits should call me *Little Rabbit*. What undeserved, or at least unknown mercies are shown to me when I am feeling trapped?

My Role in the Garden
April 24

I talked to God and asked about my role in the world.
And three deer showed up in the garden rows and they began to eat the saplings and seedlings.
I paused and watched them without malice or discontent.
Then I calmly loaded up my slingshot and I ran outside to chase them from the field.
Nothing personal, not really.

Beach Vacation After Planting Time
May 2

Blue Butterfly: Spinning flashing webs of light.
White Gull: Chortling and diving into songs.
Grey Mountain: Watching as she rises to meet the sun.
Green Ocean: Clapping, moaning and whispering the secrets of living.
Rainbow Cobble Beach: The soft round memory of a million storms.

~~~

How easy it is for a farmer
to be snagged in the sumptuous
service to a particular patch of land.
How tranquil and hard to work all day.

Come out from the heath now traveler.
Step out of your dream and rest.

When No One Buys the Harvest
May 8

I am faithful
to who shows up, and
to who does not arrive.
I am here
doing the work given to me.
This is not
what I planned.

I show up anyway.

I am here,
sculpted, hoed and tilled,
waiting for the Master's sun,
drinking the Beloved's rain,
choosing to live one more day,
stretching from the clay,
my blossoming eternally fleeting.

Make me the fruit
of your longing, God.
Make me the power
of your love, Spirits.
Make me the prosperity
of your womb, Earth.

This Day
May 15

Perhaps this is the day I am so present that no matter of doing can sway my wonder, no twisting road of thought can hide the forest, no ocean of sadness can overcome the warm sand between my toes. This is a day to remember the green bodies arching up into the sun. This is a day to say "I Love You" with a wave of my hand to the spiraling hawk. This is a day to recall how my childhood body felt when I woke up on the first morning of summer.

Even if I could do it, I still would not write your true name, God. Your name is the poem that sings the world. Instead I would move you through my skin and then talk with your voice to the sleepy bee. I'd dance the hoe through the welcoming dirt. I'd dig and find you warm and fragrant in my hand. The loam of your song falling through my fingers.

If I could breathe you in I'd become light as a dandelion's dream and float across your flowered body. Everything I know is you now. Would you like to walk with me in the round garden? Would you hold my little hand? Would you speak my true name before I die of happiness?

The Rainbird Tapping Out a Song
All I Ever Want is You
May 22

All I am is you.
This or *that*,
what are the particulars
if not you?
Voice of sparrow,
touch of dream,
jaded struggle within the garden gate,
all are you.
The barking dog,
the angry man,
the lost girl,
the kitten found beside the road,
all are you.

When i forget this
then I am not I.
Remind me, Beloved.
Let the fears be soothed
like dry clay is quenched
with the throaty song
of the sprinkler.

Watching My Wife Through the Cabin Window
For Heather
May 31

I see you on the bench drinking coffee. You watch, out there. I watch, in here. The garden is gathering her skirts all around you. You rest in the middle of a protoplasm of seed and kernel and sprout. You are a seedling dreaming her way into the light. I watch your soft tears fall to water the new growth.

Ah, love, our life is rich! Our life is so fleeting! Is our life shared from slightly different vantage points? I say "Yes!" to you and to us together! Yes to the sharing. Yes to the tear that falls sweet and light on the loving soil. This is our ground. This is our time. And we belong.

The Nice Man
June 2

He writes neat and small, concise. Controlled. He is calm as the summering dawn. He thinks good thoughts when he can. He is happy for the prosperity of the one percent, sad for the other 99. He's a good man. Honorable in how he turns in the loaded lost wallet. He makes grateful conversation with the gasoline attendant. All his ex-partners love him still, like a brother... like they always have. He smiles at the beautiful waitress, always careful never to let his eyes wander from her face. She must never see his wanting.

A secret wind blows tornadic in the back of his mouth, so he keeps himself closed, alert to shelter from the inner storm.

Here he is in his cabin, like any day, writing to God again. Or is he writing to no one? He secretly wonders. So he keeps his wondering hidden between the lines on the page. He writes with small and reasonable script, in descriptive wording and clever thoughts.

All of this to fill a book that will be seen by no one... or is that *no one* God?

He sits through another morning, just trying to be clear, drinking in the bitter grounds with the coffee's cream. He remains kind as a butler. He is free as a poet is free until the bottom of the cup is seen. When he finishes his morning, when he sets down the well-worn mug, he looks within, to the bottom. Deep down there he sees a secret field, white and drifted with stars in the shape of a dream he can longer recall.

The Worker

June 16

He works at digging,
the scraper and prier of weeds.
He works bent in the filigree mist,
mud dripping off his gloves.
He works as a scribe of the earth,
carving his scrawling script into the clay.
He works and works
until he can no longer hold
the screwdriver he uses as a weeder.
The sharp corners of tool's plastic handle
still gripped in the empty
air by his calloused hands.
He ambles to his cabin.
Then he bends into the work
at his window overlooking the farm.
He works with the impressions of light in the air.
He works with the soil still
impregnating his fingers.
But no words come, not yet.
Songs grow somewhere
in the dark,
deep in the cold mud,
beneath the sunny glade
where he lives.

Returning Home After Exile

June 7

Being a sentimental person is
both blessing and curse.
Seeing the elegant divinity in all beings, and
expecting their highest blessing of behavior
leads either to disappointment or inspiration.

For twenty years,
faithful to a family that misplaced
its shadowed sun.
Bearing a searing pain
that led me back home to myself.

I farm for sustenance,
write for sustenance,
love for sustenance,
being neither impoverished nor wealthy.

I pray I am humble and willing,
that I am the essence
of God's purpose in
this particular form of *me*.

What have I found in returning after 20 years?
A father softened with age.
A mother wizened and deepened.
A brother vulnerable,
both in his sureness and his abundant love.
I'm sure shadows still remain here.
I pray I am not one of them.

The First Harvest of the Year
June 20

The first wave of the garden
is washing out into the hungry world.
Twelve families plus one
are being fed by our handiwork tonight.
Then I think
"God, it's not enough."
And a billion voices,
like delicate copper chimes in the early dew fog,
whisper with ruffling swaying leaves.
They clear the shame of a clouded purpose, chanting:
I am sufficient.
I am sufficient.

Selling the Stuff and Jettisoning the Junk
July 4

I remembered all the stuff I saw disappear this week.
Then I forgot.
Poof, it all goes out into the world, like the cotton from a dandelion, but not so fertile.
All of it inert, like dust.

Everything we sold was just a blast of material fun, this world being an entertainment for the senses.
Then the movie ends and the material you thought was real was only a sputtering image.

My parents are edging toward the paths between the distant stars.
And this causes me to think of my allotment of days too.
Can it be that the end will really come?
This life is so many metaphors mixed together, like: *seed, dust, path.*
How poignant, fleeting and fantastic this experience is.

Love is the answer to all the pondering, dear friend.
Not the metaphor of love, but the nitty-gritty ordinary, terrifying infusion of wonder of love.

Love your life.
Love your people.
Love your land.
Love the dust and the seed.
Love the path that disappears into a field of stars.

The Garden Has Taught Me This

July 9
The chard, so wrinkled and green, speaks to me this morning.

Each plant pulls hidden nutrients up from the earth. Each soaks in the celestial light of the sun. Each strengthens its stalks in the wind. Each is a reflective product of where it sprouts, lives, blooms and dies. If seeds do not come, progeny occurs in other ways. Whatever grows will feed the gods of the garden, the ones who talk with them and walk within their rows. Whatever grows will also feed the small ones (bugs and such), their stilled plant cells becoming bodies that walk and fly.

There will be time to die in the cutting or the frost or the blight, or if one is fortunate in old age. All the living will eventually melt into the soil, becoming yet more in the coming spring. All this is occurring while feeding the secret ones (bacteria and nematodes and worms) beneath the surface.

Is our life any different from the chard's life? We see and feel in a different way. We reason. Yet within our essence we are the same. This moment, that feeling on the flesh, this kiss of the sun, that stroke of wind, this deep drink of water, that falling with the knife, this telling into the blood. All our experiences are being stored in the body and anchored deep in the mystery of earth. Perhaps we take in all we experience, akin with the chard. Our flesh, too, is stored sunlight and rain. Perhaps our beauty is ultimately meant for the distribution back into the living and the firmament.

~~~

Being a farmer has introduced ideas from the plants rising through the souls of my bare feet. The plants have offered me theories of the universe. This is one they present, so simple and resolute:

This is it!

This life, all our experiences, thoughts and dreams, this is all there is. What we take in and what we give out. What brushes by in the wind is All that we'll know in the end. And here's the warp and woof of mystery:

There is no end, only change in the changelessness.

And the tapping sprinkler sings its rain upon the leaves. I hear a song, an elaboration of the chard's theory of life:

Each experience is forever.

Isn't it amazing, a little chard can sing its theory of the universe in such poignant terms? Just think what we can sing, dear friend!

So I muse a little while longer within the waving rows of green: Though our minds are fixed on the forward progression of time, there is more. *Time*, as we know it, is illusion. It all happens at once. Unlike the chard, we just don't have the physical equipment to understand this concept yet. Even with our lost abilities, being human also has its sublime benefits. This human experience is our chance to sequentially move in a body with the focus of moment by moment.

It does not require religion or spirituality or mysticism to subscribe to the chard's view of the universe. Only physics. You can add the fluff of other metaphors if you like. I pray that what I contrive about this life ads beauty and love to the whole garden, and not to the street's burning cynicism. As for me today, I grow with the tender and ruthless touch of the Gardner. I dance in rhythm to the raven circling above. I bend to the children's feet running in circles above my roots.

This… THIS… is heaven and hell right now, right here.

Building A House Upside Down
Remodeling
August 13

Why lose the heart
in the details of technicality?
What's right?
What's wrong?
The builder scrutinizes
the unburned sticks
of the house and
forgets the hearth.

Today and Not Today
October 17

How often I look upon the garden,
seeing not the flowers,
seeing mostly work and servitude.
But not today.

Zinnia, Marigold, Astor, Cosmos, I witness you.

How often I stare into a narrow view,
so empty in this full life.
But not today.

Seeing, feeling and wonder,
these are the privileges of the living.

Ok, then I will gaze some more.
Just a little while longer.
There. How sweet.
One more look,
and then I'll be on my way.

Canning Grape Jelly and Writing Love Poems

October 21

When you work the vines,
when you cut and fertilize,
when you water and wait,
then you harvest.

When you stem and juice,
when you boil and add sweetness,
when you sterilize, fill and seal,
then you infuse the pulp and sugar together.

When you process in a rattling old pot of memory,
when you set out the jars,
when you wait for the set and click of the lids,
then the work is put aside overnight.

When you get up in the morning,
when you arrive to 50 gleaming jars of stored sun,
when you open your first jar,
then the whoosh of inward rushing sky.

You dip the spoon and find the nectar
you labored over for six months.
If the jam has not set you celebrate anyway.

Just dip the spoon in again and again.
Smile.
This is the harvest.
This is the water.
This is the sun.

Light Rain
October 22

Who lives in the light
above the clouds?
Drop by drop,
the wonder.

Here and there,
everywhere the sun
turns his gaze
into rain.

Frozen Thinking
November 15

The hard freeze finally
falls upon the land,
killing the bugs
that swamped the farm.
It's a frosty hallelujah,
at a price.
The frog,
the praying mantis,
the spider,
how did they fare?

The frost cracks open
the builders
as well as the destroyers.
Good bug,
bad bug,
who is who?

How do I protect the heart
from frozen thinking and
fearful meanderings of
a *what if* frenzy?
Suppressing one emotion
suppresses all emotions.
It's not the heart
in the cold ground
that needs rearranging,
it's the discerning
sky of the mind.

Eighth Year

Digging the Well
January 1

You will dig deep.
Then deeper.
Fortune in the placement of the blade.
The water will well up.
Turbid and muddy at first.
Then gushing.
Be still.
Wait for the clarity.
When the sweetness comes, drink deeply.

Spying on the Boy Who is Killing Something In Himself
March 30

The boy who once laughed in the swaying field of spring's wind is killing the quivering bunny.

He was down at the far end of the field.
He crept stealthy in a swale of grasses.
He thought he was unseen.
I saw.
He shot the arrow.
Then he took a stone and raised it over his head.
Smashing what lay beneath him again and again.
Whatever was happening, there was a rage involved.
Taking something for nothing.
No eating.
No meaty sustenance.
No memorial.
Fruitless.
I watched.
Impassive.
Why was I so violently afraid,
choosing only to watch?
What boy was I seeing?
And just who or what was being slain?

Islands, I Hear You Even Here
April 30

Islands, I hear you now.
Even as I dive deeper
into the field's rows and notice
the swallows taking stock
of the barn.
They too flew from a horizon far away.

How do the roots of your
mountains dive so deep?
You sing not only beneath the ocean,
but under the land of river rock and clay.

All the way here,
your voice is lifted
in the secret winds
beneath the dirt,
your songs tumbling
in the pebbles
of a thousand dreams.

Proud Sparrow
A Wedding Poem
May 1

Proud sparrow,
a little puff of big power,
huge in his cups
of liquid song.
He stands tall
on his tiny talons,
atop the cedar peak
of the house my father made,
swinging his head from side to side,
scanning the wide open field
for love and family.

He is sending arrows of song
in a wide arc of air and fire.
He hopes only in the present longing.
He captures and releases
the verses of desire.
He sings the hot sun up
through the wild rose
dripping with cold dew.

Are you happy
little big man
of air and nest?
Who waits for you
at the end of your song?

I do.

I hear you.

Bless you.

May your sun set within
a loving entanglement
of twig and moss.
May the chorus of chicks rise up
with the heat of your season on earth.

Standing in the Rows of Young Beets

At the End of the Day
May 2

The garden is
a palette of loam and clay,
resonant
with the universal song.

"Just look what I've done."
I say proudly.
"I've loved
and been loved.
Just look."

What is this Longing for Elsewhere?
June 3

What is this longing, Beloved?
An island farm today,
a desert wash of cottonwood yesterday,
a book to tell you my secrets tomorrow.
Am I alive without yearning?

What, who, why do I
want, want, want?

The love games I once played
on the fantasy islands were child's play,
child's dreams, child's comforts.
What does the man within you want?
A playground in heaven?
A heaven on earth?

Am I willing to be
your love slave
in this place right now?

I long for you here
as well as somewhere else.
The obsession with place
was misplaced.

Yet, yet…
I hear your song of islands in my body.
Are these thoughts all just imaginings?

What is wrong or right?
Nothing.
I am everywhere, love.
Just know I Am and
Ask Ask Ask.
And I will be given unto you
in your yearnings too.

I Received This Land
June 9

Every morning here at this desk,
in a cabin above a barely tamed garden,
in a land of hillbillies and angry white men.
This is the land of my exile.
I wanted an island
peopled with my peers.
I must resonate with this, here.
I received this station
in the clay worn slopes
of ignorance.
I got an island here
in the garden of weeds.

I am more alone
than I ever dreamt.
My exile is also my redemption,
in a foreign land of near poverty,
in a cresting wave upon a rolling field,
in the constant sowing
of someday soon.
I am a poet who farms,
pointing the way
to the islands of God
with a freshly harvested carrot.

Walking in the Gloaming Garden
June 19

Walking in the gloaming garden,
my skin gliding through the stillness,
orange-mauve light surrounding every being,
this body both vessel of the journey and of the stillness,
this body my home, container and confinement.

Glass walls surround my vision.
I am a lightning bug in a jar.

Nightfall comes soon.
Soon the lid will be undone.
The confinement shattered.
The glass will fall and
the light that is me will fly
into the dark.

Global Warning
July 4

The forest is so thirsty that it bows and begs to be quenched.
I sit at my desk in my air conditioned retreat and dream about the good old days to come,
somehow, somewhere.

The Barn Cat Dies
Sophie
July 9

Looking out on the field I know a thousand creatures within sight are dying right now. And a thousand more are being born to live and die. This is a poignant system you've made here, God. I know the cat was just another being, but she was one of my beings. Do you ever feel sad, God? When we die do you grieve or rejoice or worse, sit indifferent? Even if you don't feel something at all, our great and small losses are here. Even if there is a great master plan beyond the transient perception, I will feel the tears for my companion. I will feel the absence of this little one.

Everyone deserves to be accompanied and seen and held and loved when they are born. So it is when they die. God, even if you don't feel like we do, please hold our dead. Hold this little being. Be her mother and let her nuzzle and suckle and knead your tender breast.

Left the Garden Hose Running all Night
July 15

I accidently left the hose running all night in the garden.
What flood have I avoided by forgetting the water,
precious and rushing down the cabbage rows?

Last night a sad dream where she and I came home and stood apart saying:
"It's just not working out."
Foreboding today, a lingering separation of spirits from their ocean abode.
Yet the rushing water is staunched.
Maybe I flooded the garden last night just to know a muddied truth
beside the other paths so dry and hard with sun,
here in this mid-summer journey.

Waking and Weeding
Grey Sky Gray Sky Great Sky
July 16

Cool this morning.
Calm and shrouded in a misted blanket.
Slaying the fifth round of forbidden plants.
I am Shiva with sickled blade, taking the gold and green to be consumed by the fire.
I am the cold grey eye that swings the blade from on high.
Praised be the One taking me into everything,
Himself: the Sun bright and unaltered,
        just on the other side of the swirling cloud.

Wandering in the Desert
July 31

I am bedeviled by heat-waves,
then lightning flashes rise up
from the far desert.
A sweetened well of memory is opened.
The distant horizon is collecting
the billowing waters,
sending a monsoon
to this parched and barren valley,
to this brown bent farm,
in the moments to come.

Far out at sea a storm spins,
unseen by human-kind.
And yet it turns,
collecting the briny deep and
making everything in its path pure,
carrying clean water
to the desert's edge.

Within the Rabbit Proof Fence
August 11

I finally saw the creature that's been eating me up from the inside.
I have enough bounty to sustain him.
But he eats a lot of the well-tended sweetness.
Good little bunny, bad little bunny…
Longing…Craving.

Rabbit Proof Fence II
August 12

A rabbit proof fence keeps the critters in
as much as it keeps them out.
Either way the free flow
between worlds is not dammed forever.
Remember that
when you are armored and closed.

Working in the Silken Swaying Corn Rows
August 13

How much space am I taking up in the physical world?
What if I simplified the material and expanded the spiritual?

I've made a paradise that is killing me.

Small World in a Farm
August 26

I have a very small world here. A universe in three acres. I am a little god with the Gods above me
and below me. All day I labor in the garden, in the sweat of my back, in the bark of the hoe in the
dry clay, in the shred and the till. I am brought into the ultimate harvest again. I am a small universe,
shrinking and condensing, like a giant star becoming neutrons. Then going black, with a gravity so
great that not even light can escape.

The Art of Productive Waiting
August 29

I don't know what to do,
or how to proceed.
I look for signs and
feel the edge of a storm
stroke our land and
bend our forests.
But there is no real relief of rain.

Just watch, you say.
Just wait, you say.
Ok,
I'll clean my mind.
I'll shed the shoulds.
I'll speak with the air.

I live on the edge of a quenching parade.
I wait.
I watch.

Prescription for the Churning Mind
September 23

Be ye resolved
to be
     air,
to be
     water,
to be
     fire.

For the Earth is
     steady with praise.

You've soared.
You've roared.
You've flowed beneath the floor.

Cease now the struggle.
Be of one mind and many lives.
All comes together with a single prayer.

Your fields are mowed.
A simple harvest is set for your clan.
Light the fire and they will come.

See where prosperity tugs you.
Then follow the tug.

When the Singing Fades into Silence
Source Sings of a New Simplicity
October 3

In a moment this experience will be gone. Don't resist the change. What's truly *Me* survives. The words that once shined will continue to shine. Ten people, a million people, one person… whoever reads your words is within Me. Do not think yourself through the tangle of popularity. I am everywhere. And so is your creation, made together with Me. And now we continue, dying and living, breathing and decomposing, in and out. It's all the same in the end. The between is what lives forever.

Resist not the change. You've shown up for your life in Me every day, whether you knew it or not. We will walk. We will fly. We will swim in the new world. We are waiting and willing. You are in Me.

Fantasy
November 2

How many houses have I *lived* in my mind this year?
In…

> A wrecked yellow cottage in a village.
> A stripped white cabin on an ocean cliff.
> A little leaning hut in a forest glade.
> A racing rocking trailer on the open road.
> A farm of guns and glorious living breath.
> A book that breathes in electrons and breathes out bits of cosmic light.
> A pine box beneath the earth where a gold ring clatters against bone.
> A block of city lights where friends gather.

I have lived in all of these places
and no place at all,
practicing to live my dreams.
I've been a hope filled romantic,
one forbidden from entering the other world,
while looking for the wonder of elsewhere,
everywhere but here.

When I Look Outside
November 10

When I look out at the land
I actually see myself, out there.

But I tell myself:
"That's not me.
It's only the land I have poured
my life into time and time again."

I come home to this moment.
I turn my head and look into a mirror.
The face of a simple being looks back.
I see the image of one
overwrought and tired.

I tell myself:
"That's not me.
It's only the once sweet field of clover
I have tended through a long hot summer."

I know it will be time
to leave all images soon.
All the pourings and containments
cannot control the surging flood
of the river bound for the sea.

Time, the turbulent
riverbed of dreams will end.
The mirror will fall.
The field will be filled with
the soft shiny stars of the ocean.
Then who will I be?
Then…

The Night Before Losing the Farm
November 10

Late at night beside the greenhouse I built with my own hands.
A lone dog barks in the distance

Standing naked
beneath the shiny arrows of Orion.
A cold clear sky shows me eternity.
Beside me the cactus and succulents
I planted long ago in my youth,
blossom in the greenhouse.

Out here,
the shiver of the turning season runs
through my toes into the withering grass.

I ask the sky warrior two simple questions:
"Are we really leaving our home?
Is this place built for someone else?"
But only a lonely dog
in the distance barks in reply.
Then silence settles upon me with the dew.

The flowers bloom on the other side
of the protective glass
I'd set with care years ago.

I step away from the pane.
I am not so cold anymore.
I am not so sure anymore
of who or what I am.

My feet move out into the field,
into the memories I tilled and sowed
over many careful seasons.
Now a harvest of frost hovers
on this side of morning.

Is this how the exile feels
as she leaves her childhood
home of many generations?
Is this what the disenfranchised one knows
when he boards the rusted boat bound
for supposed freedom?

Is freedom really just over there,
whirling with its alluring
shards of pointed light?

Only the dog and I can guess the answer.
Perhaps his canine mind already knows
the truth about the vastness of night.
Perhaps he is already familiar
with the pang of Orion's steely gaze.
Perhaps the god of the transient
will someday tell us the secret of the eternal.
Perhaps then we can say what no one
on this cold spinning planet dares to whisper.
Perhaps we are all exiles,
with the flowers still blooming back home
in the land of our youth and our dreams.

Next Year
November 11

Another morning here at my desk.
Looking out on the misty field.
Next year the desk will only face a wall.
Next year I will look in the mirror and
still see the wide open meadow
under the blue arc of sky.

The Cat and I Wait for the Movers to Arrive
December 10

The family tree fell across
the electric lines in the storm.
The power is down.
The sump pump is stilled and
the basement is filling with water.
We are moving in a matter
of minutes.
I am crying.
All else is quiet.
No machines whirring.
No heat pumping.
Only the unchecked spring
welling up under our once
upon a time home.

Let the shift occur.
Let the home slide away.
Let the sky fall.

I am as ready as I can be.
I hear the truck rumbling up the driveway.

Just one more minute.

Let me savor the lake of silence
beneath me,
before the chaos,
before the rain begins
to flee to another country,
into another time

Aho,
me and the cat in the cabin,
waiting for the movers.
Her little private door is locked.
She is bound for an inside life now.
The field will only be hers
in dreams and memory.

Postscript

After the Move
A New Year Begins in the Condo

To Callie the Cat
January 16

Seventeen years my friend. You sit on your heated cushion. Beside me. Raising your head to meet my hand. You smile. Your eyes slant, in a trance. Your grey chin straight up, saluting the sun of my gaze. I love your purr, little kitten. I love your softness. I love your rigid insistence that we come here to write together. I love the way you run up the sun framed stairway to meet me.

You are relegated to a tiny house. Sky and field were your playground only a season ago. I wonder if you will ever play free again in the grasses? You've offered so much of yourself to be here with me. I will try to write the sky. I will endeavor to write the freedom of the spring field. I will make the pen romp after a green butterfly right here, with you. Can that ever be enough, little kitty?

Our fields are both absent and internal now. We are together in this, tethered to a chair and a box. With only a window for our little games. Crystal clarity. I love thee Kitty. The grace of necessity must hold us now. We must learn to be free, roaming around the still point of the morning.

~~~

Final Note

Callie, my sweet-loyal friend, died on the day the first proof of this book arrived at the door. For eighteen years she sat beside me and worked the fields with me. Before farming full time she was a service companion for those with psychiatric challenges. She later became a companion to my wife and children as they grew. Even more than me, she loved the fields we tended together. Now she is in those fields forever, while I only dream of them on this side of the farming life.

Friends and enlightened imperfect beings come in all sorts of shapes and sizes. On these earthly paths we walk together until our ways seemingly diverge, one through time and one into a mystery beyond and beneath all of this.

I love you small friend forever and ever. As long as I breathe I will miss thee.

Dedications

About the Author

Rick Sievers lives with his wife, Heather, on a windy hill above the Columbia River in Southwest Washington State, USA. He has worn many hats on his stubborn, dreamy head: therapist, wedding officiant, rejuvenator of houses, father, fisherman, sailor, artist and husband. He currently is focusing his vocational life on grief support work in hospice, a healing practice and writing about the joy of the seas, wind and the magic of sailing. For eight sweet, difficult years he was an organic farmer. This latest book sprang from the lovely, grueling, prosperously poor life of being a tiller of clay and nurturer of leaf. As of this writing the farm has been sold for over two years. The field is gone, and yet still brings in a harvest.

Rick Sievers
Field of Seven Houses Publishing
ricksfarm@yahoo.com
fieldofsevenhouses.blogspot.com
sailingspiritwinds.blogspot.com